TABLE OF CONTENTS

CHAPTER 1: INTRODUCTION

The purpose of this thesis is to convey how adversarial non-state actors are increasing in their number, capabilities, and operational reach; these non-state actors pose threats to the American society in ways that were previously unavailable. Approaches to counter these adversaries should be considered as an essential part of U.S. domestic and foreign policy. Further, domestic and foreign policies should be better integrated to counter these threats. This thesis will identify several gaps in current national approaches, examine some ways to mitigate these risks, and provide direction for additional exploration.

Adversarial non-state actors (NSA) discussed in this thesis cover terrorists, transnational criminal organizations (TCOs)/drug trafficking organizations (DTOs), and ideologically-driven threats. Globalization has removed previous barriers that inhibited direct coordination among these disparate NSA groups. Increasingly, there is an empowering overlap between these groups that has amplified their respective reach and capabilities. Improved technology is another factor that has enabled these groups to realize effects that in the past would have far exceeded any single group or individual's resources.

The threats posed by these NSAs run the gambit of intensity of U.S. interests, including survival, vital and peripheral.[1] Existential threats arise from the possibilities of synthetic biology and associated pandemics that could evolve from it. Well-financed terrorists groups and ideologues appear to be the greatest threat associated with pandemic risks. Vital threats are most likely to originate from cyber threats that attrite broad U.S.

---

[1] Donald Edwin Nuechterlein, *America Overcommitted: United States National Interests in the 1980s* (Lexington, KY: University Press of Kentucky, 1985), 238.

physical, fiscal, and intellectual environments. Important threats that focus on killing and destroying localized physical property are most likely to arise from less capable terrorists groups and lone-wolf actors. While some terrorists have less immediate destructive power, risks exist for even them to damage the national psyche and alter the U.S. way of life. Social disruption resulting from terrorists attacks can be as harmful, and at times, even more harmful to national security than the original attack. The author examines economics and supply chain disruption in this thesis to illustrate the threats from cascading failures.

The United States' enduring interests of security, economic prosperity, and maintaining U.S. values are all targets of the aforementioned non-state actors. The U.S. government at all levels desires mitigating risks from these threat actors. However, current policy approaches give little consideration to the American populace as a means of strength and prevention. Whereas the Federal Emergency Management Agency (FEMA) directly engages the U.S. populace to mitigate risks associated with natural disasters, little effort has been applied to use the same populace as a source of strength against the nation's non-state-actor threats. Given the current resource constraints in the federal budget and an increasing national debt, the populace could offer current-government approaches a low cost opportunity to reduce the risks posed by non-state adversaries. After all, the populace is often immediately present at the point of attack, even if they are not the target themselves.

Total risk mitigation from non-state actors is unlikely but further reduced risk levels are achievable through the concept of resilience. Resilience is a term increasingly used in current national policies, and can be generally defined as pro-action before potential attacks instead of merely fortitude to weather an attack when it occurs. Current Homeland Security policy uses a nearly exclusive top down approach to protecting the American citizen. This approach under-utilizes available resources and creates unnecessary security gaps. The U.S. homeland is an operational environment; U.S. security approaches should treat it as one and include the populace to help secure it. The U.S. government should consider employing a more comprehensive or full-spectrum approach that includes the U.S. populace in a bottom-up approach to bolster on-going homeland security efforts as part of the larger effort to secure U.S. national security. After all, the threat's capabilities and capacities are growing and the government's resources to mitigate them appear to be increasingly constrained.

CHAPTER 2: RISE OF THE NON-STATE THREAT ACTORS (NSA)

> "Our terrorist adversaries and the tactics and techniques
> they employ are evolving rapidly. We will see new
> attempts, and likely successful attacks."[1] -The Bi-Partisan
> Policy Center

Non-State Threat Actors (NSA) are stateless organizations and individuals who are ungoverned by international law, yet possess the capability and capacity to harm the enduring interests of the United States. Some examples of these actors are terrorists, transnational criminal organizations (TCO), and ideologues that have crossed purposes with the United States' goals. Terrorists use violence as a means to achieve a desired political end state. TCOs are primarily profit driven; when violence enlarges their profits, their violence also grows. Various respective convictions drive ideologues, and violence often accompanies those convictions. Increasingly, these groups are beginning to overlap in their interactions. Although these disparate groups seek different long-term goals, sharing their respective means often increases the strength of all involved.

Increased Globalization

NSAs enlarged their stature as "globalization" began in the early 1990s. Globalization is represented in the novel spreading and connecting of people, ideas, merchandise, products, and information that previously was unfounded. These newfound exchanges profited many in the West and offered new export markets to the less developed world. Other positive results of globalization are the growth of knowledge that was previously held by elites or simply unconsidered. This new environment drove an awakening in underdeveloped regions as they became aware of their wealth disparity compared to the industrial world. While adaptive cultures leveraged globalization to

---

[1] Lee Hamilton and Thomas Kean, *Tenth Anniversary Report Card the Status of the 9/11 Commission Recommendations* (Washington, D.C.: Bipartisan Policy Center, 2011), 7.

increase their wealth by embracing newly realized and superior methods, more traditional societies often felt threatened by the exposure to new ideas that countered their customary way of life. These traditional societies often shunned globalization and withdrew further.

Globalization brought more than new cultural ideas with it. New awareness of perceived oppression and injustices reopened grievances that ignorance had been left dormant. Further, new technologies brought in new capabilities that empowered those who held them. Capabilities such as anti-air missiles, anti-tank mines and sophisticated communication equipment that once were exclusively the domain of states were quickly becoming commonplace among independent groups within state borders. When traditional societies felt their customs threatened, some embraced this newly-learned and lethal knowledge to push back the cultural inflows that challenged their traditional way of life.[2]

The CCJO for 2020 states that in the future "The diffusion of advanced technology in the global economy means that middleweight militaries and non-state actors can now muster weaponry once available only to superpowers."[3] Added to these groups' expanded lethal capabilities, they also have gained expanded capacities through globalized networks that move funds, information, ideas, weapons and people across borders affording them an unprecedented level of influence.

During the same period, drug trafficking organizations, transnational criminal organizations and ideologically based terror organizations began reaching out towards

---

[2] Keith Dickson, PhD., *Justifying War in a Globalized World: Problems and Prospects* (Norfolk, VA: National Defense University, 2011), 4.

[3] U.S. Joint Chiefs of Staff, *Capstone Concept for Joint Operations 2020* (Washington, D.C.: Government Printing Office, 2012), 24.

one another, seeking transactional cooperation to pursue their individual interests.[4]

Terrorist organizations can now communicate their ideology, recruit, and train individuals through the internet. Operational information could now be digitally encrypted and easily shared. Cyberspace can help mask identities through a number of obscurant methods. Globalization allowed freer travel across national borders – both legally and illegally. Regional criminal actors have used globalization to expand into transnational criminal organizations (TCO).[5] TCOs are able to function as multi-national corporations that move illicit tonnages of narcotics, weapons, and human cargoes throughout the world using established and expanding networks. This collusion of disparate actors working towards near term goals has been termed "commodification".[6] Commodification addresses the illicit outsourcing of some needed capacities in order for the group to focus better on its enduring goals. Trafficking, security and logistics are organizational requirements commonly outsourced in today's globalization.

Non-state actors operate primarily in "hollow states," where local governance is weak, yet its resident state's sovereignty is still internationally recognized. Some examples are: Al Qaeda in Pakistan, Afghanistan, Yemen, Sudan, and Mali; Hizballah in Lebanon; and, FARC in Venezuela. Sometimes the state allows this presence; sometimes the state simply has no capacity to affect NSAs. These sanctuaries often act as a proving ground to these actors where they grow in strength and boldness.

Access to Improving Technology

---

[4] Moisés Naím, *Illicit: How Smugglers, Traffickers and Copycats are Hijacking the Global Economy* (New York: Doubleday, 2005),150.

[5] John Sullivan, "Counter-Supply and Counter-Violence Approaches to Narcotics Trafficking," *Small Wars & Insurgencies* 21, no. 1 (2010), 179.

[6] Phillip Bobbitt, *Terror and Consent: The Wars for the Twenty-First Century* (New York, N.Y.: Alfred A, Knopf, 2008), 672.

The Federal Bureau of Investigation (FBI) threat model is built upon a metaphorical three-legged stool that expresses three essential elements that must be extant for the stool to stand and pose a viable threat. These three threat elements are: intent or willingness to commit an illegal act; the technical capacity to perform the act; and lastly, the capability (similar to operational reach) to commit the act. Malicious intent among non-state actor adversaries is inherent by definition. Technology is empowering NSA's capabilities through the acquisition of new electronic tools and technical means that were previously unavailable or unaffordable. Lastly, collusion (afforded by globalization) empowers non-state actor capacities through networking. NSA threat examples are illustrated in the following chapter.

Moore's Law

The information revolution, most specifically illustrated by the increasing expansion of computing capacity all the while reducing in both size and price, has been a true enabler for the NSA. Charting this trend is a principle known as *Moore's Law*,[7] seen in Figure 1. The availability of increasingly capable and affordable electronics allows newfound abilities, once only affordable by nation states, into the hands on non-state actors. As an illustration, the computer system that took Apollo 12 to the moon is several orders-of-magnitude less capable than even the first generation iPhone. Apple recently sold over five million of their new fifth generation iPhone.[8]

---

[7] Columbia Electronic Encyclopedia, *Moore's Law*, Vol. 6th Edition: Columbia University Press, 2011, 1-1.

[8] Joshua Freed, "IPhone 5 Sales: Many U.S. Stores Reportedly Sold Out of the Device Already," *Huffington Post*, September 12, 2012.

Photo Removed Due to Copyright Restrictions

Figure 1- Exponential Growth of Computing Capacity over Time. [9]

Concrete examples of Moore's Law can be found in typical smart phones that increasingly more people own and leverage. Merely five years ago, global positioning systems, cellular phones, and MP3 players were all distinctly different electronic devices that cost over $100 each. Today all of these capabilities are subsumed into the single platform of a single smart phone. Low-end smart phones are regularly offered today at $99 with a cellular service plan. Non-state actors routinely use cheap cellular devices to detonate precisely executed improvised explosive devices against their adversaries. Other examples of expanded technology include Lebanese Hizballah use of unmanned aerial vehicles against the Israeli Defense Forces and Mexican drug trafficking

---

[9] D. K. Burke, "Moore's Law Graph," http://www.dreamviews.com, http://www.dreamviews.com/f77/moores-law-there-limit-98762/ (accessed October 29, 2012).

8

organizations use of night vision devices to avoid U.S. Customs and Border Patrol teams.[10]

Increased knowledge and C2 devices

Individuals today are able to acquire actionable information that was just recently far from reach. Google Earth affords general routing and travel information as well as specific street level views that afford high-fidelity terrain orientation. One can now reconnoiter their targets without physically visiting the target site.[11] This capability benefits operational security of the adversary planner by affording them rehearsals without risks of physical presence. Questions about most any topic can be located on-line at places like Wikipedia for a general level of learning, and more detailed sites like GoogleScholar and GoogleBooks afford venues for in depth research. People's individual biographies and even current locations can be determined through Facebook, LinkedIn, and other social media sites. Situational awareness and synchronized communications with targeted masses is afforded through Twitter. Flickr has been used to share real time digital images with the world at large and convey all the information and emotion that a picture can. Sometimes these images move masses to action as witnessed during the Arab Spring uprisings.[12] The term fauxtography arose in 2006 from Hizballah efforts to control the narrative with altered photos. These images are generally

---

[10] Gil Hoffman, "'Hezbollah Drone Photographed Secret IDF Bases'," Jerusalem Post, http://www.jpost.com/Defense/Article.aspx?id=287724 (accessed December 13, 2012).

[11] Groundspeak Incorporated, "Groundspeak's Geocaching Application," , http://www.geocaching.com/live/ (accessed October 29, 2012, October 29, 2012).

[12] Essam Mansour, "The Role of Social Networking Sites (SNSs) in the January 25th Revolution in Egypt," *Library Review* 61, no. 2 (2012), 128.

altered in an effort to motivate the viewer in a given direction.[13] Protestors used these technology tools to maximize their protest's effectiveness during the G8 Summits and Arab Spring.[14] The Bahraini government blocked their citizens' access to these websites and social-media tools during their recent riots.[15] This government prohibition somewhat limited the sizes and effectiveness of counter-government riots held in their capital city- Manama.[16]

The ability of technology to manage one's life, calendars, and information flows has extended beyond personal use into command and control capabilities as well. Non-state actors have used these technologies for their operational control to great effectiveness. Terrorists, anarchists, and criminal organizations have all been documented using these technologies for nefarious ends.[17] Examples of this advantage will be further discussed in Chapter 3.

Synthetic Biology (Carlsson's Curve)

One area of science that has realized significant increases from technology is synthetic biology; this technology is quickly coming into the reach of NSAs. Much the way that Moore's Law charts the increasing computer capacity and decreasing costs, Carlsson's Curve documents the costs per base pair of DNA sequencing and synthesis. The cost is now within the range of many scientists to sequence DNA pairs into a form

---

[13] Danielle Mastropiero, "Hezbollah Uses Fauxtography to Sway Public," International Media Ethics, http://www.imediaethics.org/News/411/Hezbollah_uses_fauxtography_to_sway_public_.php (accessed October 30, 2012).

[14] Sean Aday, *Blogs and Bullets II New Media and Conflict After the Arab Spring* (Washington, D.C.: United States Institute of Peace, 2012), 5.

[15] Bahraini-Shia citizens protested against their standing Sunni- monarchy in the 2011 Pearl Uprisings/Pearl Revolution.

[16] Freedom House, "Freedom on the Net: Bahrain," Freedom House, http://www.freedomhouse.org/report/freedom-net/2012/bahrain (accessed October 29, 2012).

[17] Naím, Illicit: How Smugglers, Traffickers and Copycats are Hijacking the Global Economy, 102.

that replicates other organisms found in nature or even create new-novel organisms not

currently found in nature. Before synthetic biology, sequencing required an actual

physical specimen from nature. Today, this sequencing can be done with no original

DNA material. The term for this function is *de novo* or from nothing. Viruses are among

the many natural organisms that can be synthetically replicated. The essential hardware

required for this sequencing is available for sale on line and is regularly advertised for

under $50,000.[18] Costs have historically been limiting factors in viral threat scenarios,

and only nation states could previously afford a viral program. However, the current

price point is clearly within the reach of many non-state actor adversaries.

Most recently, knowledge has limited non-state actors from acquiring viral threat

capabilities. However, another non-state actor, academia, has afforded new prospects to

the nation's adversaries. No collusion or malice was involved in transferring this

knowledge but the capability was afforded to NSAs all the same. Recently academic

institutions fully mapped the 1918 H1N1 (Spanish influenza epidemic) and the H5N1

(bird influenza) virus genomes.[19] These two viruses are notable in that the 1918 version,

H1N1, was extremely virulent and led to the death of millions, but only had mortality

rates in the 3 percent range. The bird flu, H5N1, is generally found only in birds but has

occasionally jumped species into humans. H5N1 has less virulence than typical

influenzas (including H1N1 variants) but has a mortality rate of ~ 60 percent once it

transfers to humans.[20] Further, researchers have identified which sections of these

---

[18] Certified Genetool, "For Sale: ABI 3900 Oligo (DNA) Synthesizer," http://www.labx.com, http://www.labx.com/v2/adsearch/detail3.cfm?adnumb=481442 (accessed November 8, 2012).

[19] John Cohen and Martin Enserink, "One of Two Hotly Debated H5N1 Papers Finally Published," ScienceNow, http://news.sciencemag.org/sciencenow/2012/05/one-of-two-hotly-debated-h5n1-pa.html (accessed September 4, 2012).

[20] Eric Allely, M.D., *National Response to Biologic Contagion: Lessons from Pandemic Planning* (Suffolk, Virginia: Joint Center for Operational Analysis, 2008), 12.

respective virus genomes cause their high virulence and high mortality. Those same scientists made that virulence and mortality information publicly available via the internet. This readily accessible information now affords a capable person with the ingredients to build dangerous novel viruses from nothing. This new knowledge combined with reducing equipment prices and menacing intentions could spark an epidemic to cripple a nation, region, or beyond.

CHAPTER 3: NON-STATE THREAT ACTOR TECHNIQUES

This chapter will discuss terrorists, ideologues, and transnational criminal organizations that pose threats to America's enduring interests. To inform the reader, the author uses overviews and historical examples for each actor type to amplify the capabilities these threats possess.

Terrorists and their Attacks

Terrorism is not a new concept. It has been used as long as men have struggled with one another. Terrorism is not even new to America; one should recall recent historical examples such as the Ku Klux Klan, the Weathermen, and Black Panthers. However, since the al-Qaeda (AQ) attacks of September 11, 2001, contemporary terrorism is most often associated with radical Islam and this section discusses three leading Islamist terror groups from both Shia and Sunni sects.

Lebanese Hizballah (LH) – "Army of God"

> …top intelligence officials and leaders told the Majority's investigative staff that Hezbollah is the group most capable of flipping its nationwide network of criminal fundraising cells into an operational terror force capable of great violence on orders from its leaders in Lebanon or Iran. And in 2009, the Obama Administration said that Hezbollah is "the most technically capable terrorist group in the world.[1] Congressman Peter King, N.Y., March 12, 2012

Lebanese Hizballah (LH) is the world's leading Shia terrorist group. Specifying "Lebanese" Hizballah is important because they have franchised their organization among the Lebanese diaspora around the world. These franchises offer financial, moral and at least logistics support in their locales. Concern exists that their franchises might

---

[1] House Committee on Homeland Security, Hearing: on "Iran, Hezbollah, and the Threat to the Homeland," 112th Cong., 2nd sess., 2012, 4.

provide direct operational support. The most prolific franchises can be found in the United States, South America, and West Africa but others are located throughout Europe and the Middle East as well.[2] LH was founded in 1980 when members of the Iranian Revolutionary Guards Corps – Quds Force arrived on a flight into Lebanon and began organizing, training, and equipping LH to be a proxy force. LH is a split-off organization from the Amal movement that fought for Shia causes against the Sunni and Christian militias during the 1980s Lebanese civil war.

Cast in the light of the Iranian revolution, LH is focused on Shia dominance of Lebanon and has a secondary goal of Israel's destruction. Israel's invasion of Beirut in 1982 reinforced LH's zeal. Although significant LH funding comes from Iran, still other significant funding comes from LH's work in illicit activities around the world.[3] LH has been involved in smuggling blood diamonds from Africa, narcotics in South America, and arbitrage schemes in America ranging from franchise infringement to cigarette tax leveraging between U.S. states.[4]

LH's capability has soared through the lucrative funding sources and training from Iran. While LH is clearly the strongest military force in Lebanon,[5] they may actually be the strongest Arab military force in the Middle East. In 2006, Hizballah made a strategic and unanticipated mistake when they attacked and kidnapped Israeli Defense Force (IDF) members along the Lebanon/Israeli border. The ensuing conflict quickly escalated to a significant war that displayed LH's capabilities. In retaliation to IDF air

---

[2] Tom Diaz and Barbara Newman , *Lightning Out of Lebanon: Hezbollah Terrorists on American Soil* (New York: Ballantine Books, 2005), 4.

[3] Naím, Illicit: How Smugglers, Traffickers and Copycats are Hijacking the Global Economy, 142.

[4] Diaz and Newman, 86.

[5] Middle East Reporter, "United Lebanese Army: Attempts to Keep it so," *Middle East Reporter (Weekly Edition)* 137, no. 1227 (11/06, 2010), 15.

strikes, LH halted IDF armored columns and ground forces with the novel use of anti-tank guided missiles (ATGMs). They struck and nearly sank the IDF flagship, the Hinnant, with a C-802 anti-ship cruise missile. Throughout the conflict, they launched a withering barrage of Katusha missiles into northern Israel, and they sustained that firing volume even until the last day when the truce was established. LH, a non-state actor, withstood the attack of the region's most powerful military power and stymied their advances. Their "win by not losing"[6] strategy accomplished what Arab state armies had failed to accomplish in 1948, 1967 and 1973. LH proved that the IDF was not invincible and that realization greatly eroded Israel's deterrence capability.

Knowing that Hizballah has franchises around the globe and that they have even greater capacity today than when they successfully attacked Israeli related targets in Argentina in 1994[7], the U.S. should pay close attention to this threat. Their illicit activities bring them into direct contact with organized crime and its associated logistic and operational capacities. Law enforcement officials have stated that Hizballah "support cells"[8] are active in at least 15 major U.S. cities.[9] Given the illicit tonnage that organized crime successfully smuggles into the U.S. every year, one can easily understand how LH could smuggle in a load of ATGMs, or man portable air-defense systems instead of routine marijuana loads. Further, specially trained LH operators can mask their ingress into the US with illegal aliens or other smuggling operations.

---

[6] Terence Trenchard, *Hezbollah in Transition: Moving from Terrorism to Political Legitimacy* (Carlisle Barracks, PA: U.S. Army War College, 2011), 21-30.

[7] In 1994, Hizballah attacked Jewish community targets located inside Argentina. The attacks killed 85 people.

[8] Lebanese diaspora often have been approached to give funding for LH charities in Lebanon. While these collection groups are logistically supportive, law enforcement routinely declines to classify them as operationally supportive. Support Cells are enablers not operatorives.

[9] House Committee on Homeland Security Subcommittee on Counterterrorism and Intelligence, *Hezbollah in the Western Hemisphere*, 112th Cong., 2nd sess., 2012, 3.

Lashkar-e-Taiba (LeT) – "Army of the Pure"

LeT is a Sunni terrorist group that is similar to LH in that it sometimes acts as a proxy force for a state actor, Pakistan. Pakistan's Inter-Services Intelligence (ISI) section is the state's premier intelligence wing.[10] It has used proxies in the past, and some sources state Pakistan regularly uses proxy forces to shape and fight the nation's battles. These proxy forces intimidate Pakistan's adversaries while affording them deniability; their use has also kept the country from becoming directly engaged in a state-on-state conflict.[11]

Pakistan sees India as its nemesis and this angst links back to the partition of the two countries based on disparate religions. Pakistan formed by gathering Muslims for protection into western India, while the Hindus in western India moved eastward seeking the relative protection among other Hindus in India. These migrations ultimately resulted in the separation of Pakistan from India. The tensions between these two faiths are considerable and that tension carries over at the state level.[12] Mumbai is the economic capital of India, and in 2008, LeT conducted a "complex attack"[13] there. LeT disrupted India's sense of normalcy and security. The attack's psychological effects were significant, perhaps more significant than the attack itself.

---

[10] Chidanand Rajghatta, "Rana, Headley Implicate Pak, ISI in Mumbai Attack during ISI Chief's Visit to US," *Times of India*, April 12, 2011.

[11] Lawrence J. Korb and Alexander Rothman, "No First use: The Way to Contain Nuclear War in South Asia," *Bulletin of the Atomic Scientists* 68, no. 2 (March 2012), 34, http://ezproxy6.ndu.edu/login?url=http://search.ebscohost.com/login.aspx?direct=true&db=aph&AN=72475126&site=ehost-live&scope=site.

[12] Robert D. Kaplan , *Monsoon: The Indian Ocean and the Future of American Power* (New York, N.Y.: Random House, 2010), 374-84.

[13] A complex attack describes a military style assault with more than a single type of weapon system organized into a coherent combined-arms effect on the target. LeT's Mumbai attack used explosives, direct-fire weapons, fire and psychlogicical operations.

LeT's attackers were uneducated Muslim youth that had been recruited from

Pakistan's streets. LeT, with direct ISI support, indoctrinated and trained these youth for

a specific raid mission on Mumbai. Counter terrorism experts broadly agree that the

Mumbai attack showed new destruction capabilities with complex attacks traits. "This

was a lot more like a Special Forces raid than any terrorist attack we've seen to date."[14]

The group of youth used the cover name "Deccan Mujahedeen" as part of their

psychological operations. Decca is a large central plain in India and having the Indian

populace believe that the attack on their homeland came from within increased the

potential psychological impacts. Technology also increased the operational reach of both

the attackers and their controllers who remotely guided them from within Pakistan.

The initial reconnoiter of Mumbai's targeted sites was done by a Caucasian

American, David Headly, who had recently converted to Islam. NYPD's report on

radicalization illustrated how new converts are often the most zealous members because

they are eager to prove their loyalties.[15] Headly did not profile as a Muslim, which

provided him easier access and less scrutiny from Indian security forces. The actual

attackers had never physically seen their targets. Instead, they used "commodification"

and a series of commercially-available technologies that empowered them to near Special

Operations Force abilities.[16] Google Earth afforded the raiders with an overview of

Mumbai and the selected targets. The website's street view application allowed the

youths to get a sense of the city and land marks without actually being there. Using

---

[14] David Kilcullen, "Counterterrorism Blog Panel: The 2008 Mumbai Attacks" December 4, 2008, http://counterterrorismblog.org/upload/2008/12/The%202008%20Mumbai%20Attacks_CTB%20Event%20 12.04.08.pdf (accessed August 30, 2012).

[15] Mitchell D. Silber and Arvin Bhatt, *Radicalization in the West the Homegrown Threat* (New York, N.Y.: New York Police Dept., 2007), 29.

[16] Middle East Reporter, United Lebanese Army: Attempts to Keep it So.

piracy operations, the raiding force of ten overtook a fishing trawler and killed all the crew except for the captain. They forced the captain to navigate the vessel lengthy distances from Pakistan into Indian waters near Mumbai. Once nearer their destination, the captain was executed and the team simply used GPS to "drive" the ship into harbor.

After arriving in the port, the group split into five separate raiding teams and conducted a "complex attack" that simultaneously prosecuted their assigned targets. Police were quickly overwhelmed by the assault team's firepower. While the attackers had preplanned and preloaded numerous magazines for their fully automatic AK-47s, the Indian police were generally equipped with a lathi, a four foot-long bamboo baton. Fewer still had World War II vintage single shot rifles, many without any ammunition.[17] One of the assault teams added chaos and confusion to its destruction after it commandeered a police car and struck targets from it.

These particular attacks created chaos and fear among the Indian populace. The five groups used cell phones to coordinate horizontally with each other as they simultaneously assaulted their targets; they used satellite phones to coordinate vertically with controllers in Pakistan. The attackers used fire as an additional tool of terror as they moved from one targeted location to the next. While Indian first responders were trying to contain the death and fire destruction at one site, the attackers moved on to prosecute new targets. People and property were key targets. Jews and Westerners were the primary human targets but murdered Indians were also valued. The attackers watched local television broadcasts to improve their situational awareness of Indian security force

---

[17] Tom Monahan and Mark Stainbrook, "Learning from the Lessons of the 2008 Mumbai Terrorist Attacks," *Police Chief.* 78, no. 2 (2011), 25.

movements. These broadcasts reduced the security forces' element of surprise and strengthened the attackers' lethality.

When fortitude waned among one raiding-terror team, controllers from Pakistan implored the shooter to go execute the Jews in the next room. "Kill them now!" was the command.[18]

Intercepted communications, now made available to the public, record the fatal shot and the affirmation and congratulations of the controller from afar. When the end of mission was near and the attackers' culmination was apparent to the controllers, they directed the attackers to reserve several full clips and a few hand grenades for use against the Indian assault force they were watching closing-in via television. Inflicting the maximum damage possible before their own demise was their goal from the beginning.[19] This tactic will be discussed later in active shooter scenarios.

The significance of the Mumbai attacks is that it shows how globalization empowered simple street thugs afforded with less than six months of specialized training, equipped with off-the-shelf technology and excess military grade weapons were able to consume the entire security force apparatus of a nuclear-armed state for three days. Numerous land-marked buildings were damaged and over 160 people were killed during the attacks. Both national pride and government legitimacy all atrophied because of this attack.

---

[18] Associated Press, "Phone Transcripts of Mumbai Attacks Indicate Gunmen Not Acting Alone," Fox News, www.foxnews.com/story/0,2933,477424,00.html (accessed Oct 29, 2012).

[19] Angel Rabasa, *The Lessons of Mumbai* (Santa Monica, CA: RAND Corp., 2009), 31.

Al-Qaeda (AQ) – The Base

Al-Qaeda is the final illustrated terrorism example. AQ is a Sunni terrorist group with Salafists ideals that are Jihadi at its core.[20] AQ is a globalization example where ideological, criminal and political motivations overlap. Where the previously two discussed groups had some nation state sponsorship, AQ has often worked inside and from established nation states but generally without direct support. Although not directly government supported, AQ has received passive support from several governments and local leaders. Due to its religious convictions, this group's cadre can be viewed as non-deterrable. Numerous suicide attacks reinforce this view. When AQ declared a Holy War upon the United States in 1998, few Americans noticed but this ignorance would soon change.

AQ attacked America on September 11, 2001 and used novel approaches to kill over 3,000 people across three U.S. states. They leveraged the nation's own assets, capabilities, and freedoms to their advantage. They raised money from charities and individual donors to finance their operations, and operated within a U.S. self-imposed intelligence seam that limited information sharing between U.S. internal and external intelligence agencies.[21]

AQ is not a group of members as much as it is an idea where other like-minded Salafist terrorists can gather and act. National regimes or parts of regimes have sheltered the group's leadership across the globe from Sudan, Afghanistan, and Pakistan. According to a Brookings Institute paper, Iran has even afforded sanctuary to AQ because the two groups found a common

---

[20] Salifists are Muslim fundamentalists who prescribe to a strict life style of following the prophet Mohammed. Jihadi Salafists use violence to persuade others to also follow their prescribed views of living. Jihadis sometime even see their attacks as a religious imperative.

[21] Project on National Security Reform and Center for the Study of the Presidency, "*Forging a New Shield*," Center for the Study of the Presidency, Project on National Security Reform, 79.

enemy in the U.S..[22] While AQ is a non-state actor, it regularly hits with the full force of a

nation state.

AQ has been attacking the United States since the 1990s up to the writing of this thesis

and no cessation appears imminent. The original 1993 bombing of the World Trade Center

towers had ideological linkages to AQ. That attack's mastermind, "the Blind Sheik," had ties

back to the AQ deputy Zawahiri and the Muslim Brotherhood in Egypt. AQ has attacked U.S.

Embassies in Tanzania, Kenya; current as of this writing, their franchised forces killed the U.S.

Ambassador in Libya, Ambassador J. Christopher Stevens on September 11, 2012. His death

marks the first U.S. Ambassador killed in the line of duty since 1979.[23]

AQ has regularly used asymmetric approaches in its attacks. They gather funding

on-line and through dubious charities. Their July 7, 2005, London attacks exchanged

narcotics for needed explosives. They used their targets' resources against them and

created a branding through the media and internet forums. Their message attracts

disgruntled and passionate like-minded groups to adopt their ideology and adapt their

tactics. AQ has adeptly used the internet to proselytize and train its new recruits; these

new recruits are often quite zealous to prove their loyalties, and recruiters often use these

converts in their most brazen attacks.[24]

While airlines have been a key weapons system for AQ—9/11, the Shoe Bomber,

the Underwear Bomber, and parcel bombs from Yemen—they also have pursued other

tools of destruction. Biological and chemical weapons are stated pursuits, and bin Laden

---

[22] Bruce Reidel, "The Al Qaeda-Iran Connection," Brookings Institute, http://www.brookings.edu/research/opinions/2011/05/29-al-qaeda-riedel (accessed October 29, 2012).
[23] Geoff Dyer, "US Bolsters Security After Libya Raid," *Financial Times*, http://www.ft.com/cms/s/0/e8d91afe-fc53-11e1-aef9-00144feabdc0.html (accessed October 29, 2012).
[24] Eric Schmitt, "Aafia Siddiqui," *New York Times*, September 24, 2010, http://topics.nytimes.com/top/reference/timestopics/people/s/aafia_siddiqui/index.html (accessed October 14, 2012).

declared the acquisition of nuclear weapons as a religious imperative. Even when

considering the virility of the AQ Khan network,[25] non-state nuclear ambitions are lofty.

However, weaponized fissile materials, wastes from nuclear medicine, and resultant dirty

bombs are at a lower and more attainable threshold for an attack success. Any of these

weaponized materials packaged into radiological dispersal devices (RDDs) could cause

significant social disruption and economic damage.

Chemical weapons and biological weapons are increasing threats worth U.S.

efforts to deter and interdict. Before the fall of the Taliban, AQ created poison gas

intended for use on humans. The group proved its weapon's viability to the world by

releasing a film of its lethal use on animals.[26] More recently, AQ's graduate-level,

American-educated neuroscientist, Afia Siddiqui[27] was arrested in Afghanistan. She is a

graduate of both Massachusetts Institute of Technology and Brandeis University.[28] Her

capture timing was fortuitous because she was removed from AQ's services shortly

before academics published revealing genome data for both H5N1 and H1N1 viruses.[29]

A person with the graduate level training and access to synthetic biology equipment

could use that recently released information to work towards nefarious ends. Any

successes in those endeavors would pose significant dangers to populaces around the

world.

---

[25] AQ Khan is the Pakistani physicist that worked covertly to proliferate nuclear weapons designs and methods for Pakistan and is often referred to as the father of the "Islamic Bomb" after Pakistan used his supplied information to build its first nuclear weapon.

[26] Judith Miller, "Qaeda Videos seem to show Chemical Tests," *New York Times*, August 19, 2002. 1.

[27] Afia Siddiqui is a well-trained graduate level scientist who offered her services to AQ. She was apprehended in Afghanistan and later shot one of her subduers to avoid detention.

[28] Schmitt, "Aafia Siddiqui", 1.

[29] Cohen and Enserink, "One of Two Hotly Debated H5N1 Papers Finally Published," *Science Now Magazine*, May 2, 2012, http://news.sciencemag.org/sciencenow/2012/05/one-of-two-hotly-debated-h5n1-pa.html.

Ideologues and their Attacks

Convictions motivate ideologues to action. These actors can be among the most dangerous because they are often undeterrable. Their actions can be viewed as irrational because their paradigms often do not match the main stream. Deterrence is weak against these actors because they feel both validation in their successes and the need for vindication by their failures; the result is that each of their attacks will ultimately reinforce their zeal to continue further attacks. The advent of rapid technology advances can make these ideologues "super-empowered individuals" that cause much greater damage than a single person could in the past. The following section will deal with three ideological examples: Aum Shinrikyo, Cyber Warriors, and Ted Kaczynski.

Aum Shinrikyo

Aum Shinrikyo was a messianic and apocalyptic cult centered in Japan through the 1980s and 1990s. Its leader, Shoko Asahara, declared himself the "enlightened one" and led his technically savvy followers to seclude themselves from the populace. This isolation screened any counter messaging that might oppose his goals. This separation began a radicalization of Aum Shinrikyo recruits and instilled in them an "us and them" mindset. "Them," the outside world who did not convert as the followers had, were cast as unworthy and doomed to fate at the organization's hands.[30]

The first documented Aum Shinrikyo attack was a botched anthrax attack on the neighborhood surrounding their compound. Scientists from the group mistakenly acquired a strain of anthrax benign to humans and used their technical prowess to reproduce these benign spores in significant quantities. They acquired anthrax through

---

[30] Holly Fletcher, *Aum Shinrikyo*: Council on Foreign Relations, http://www.cfr.org/japan/aum-shinrikyo/p9238 (accessed September 12, 2012).

legal-commercial means and the reproduction was done in house but out of sight of the broader Japanese community.[31]

The attack was conducted by dispersing the anthrax spores from an elevated chimney during a damp day with light winds. Infectant saturation of the targeted area was near ideal. The surrounding community complained of the smell coming from their compound and called the police to investigate. Police inquired of the cult at their compound who explained they were performing a spiritual cleansing ritual and that the police could not enter. Since Japanese law protects religious freedom and practices, the police departed. The cult continued dispersing the material after the police departed. The total time of anthrax dispersal lasted for nearly two days, until the cult ran out of spores. Fortunately, the strain did not harm humans but did kill numerous birds and other animals in the affected dispersal zone.[32]

> The cult was adept at recruiting educated professionals (scientists and engineers), but most were young and largely inexperienced. Camp Satyan 7 was designed to produce sarin, not on a small terrorist scale, but in nearly battlefield quantities: thousands of kilograms a year.[33]

The next attack perpetrated by the cult was a sarin gas attack on the Tokyo subway system. The attack profile was similar to their earlier attack in that they created their weapon system in house and their target was the broader Japanese populace. The Tokyo subway system is among the heaviest used subway systems in the world. Cult members loaded the liquid sarin poison into plastic soda bottles and targeted subway routes near government buildings. Before departing their subway cars, the operatives

---

[31] Kyle Olson, "Aum Shinrikyo: Once and Future Threat?" *Emerging Infactious Diseases* Volume 5, no. Number 4 (August 1999, 1999).

[32] U.S. Joint Chiefs of Staff, Joint Staff J-7, *Super Empowered Threat Brief* (Suffolk, VA: Joint Center for Operational Analysis, 2008), 14.

[33] Olson, 2.

punctured these containers allowing the sarin to leak out onto the floor and off-gas.[34]

While the poison killed less than 20 people and injured several hundreds of others, several thousand Japanese sought medical treatment and quickly overwhelmed the modern Japanese medical system. Although most were only "worried well,"[35] hospitals admitted over 1000 citizens and eventually 47 Japanese survivors were certified by their government as permanently disabled.[36] Psychological effects from this attack affected the entire city instead of just those in the immediate area. Psychological effects will be discussed in greater detail in the next chapter.

Cyber Threats

Cyber threats are another increasing risk to the American way of life. A key financial sector leader interviewed for Bob Woodward's book, *Obama's War stated,* "If the attackers on 9/11 had been cyber-savvy and attacked a single bank, it would have been an order of magnitude greater damage to the U.S. and global economies than dropping both World Trade Towers."[37] While many writers have chosen to title or categorize the cyber threat actors in ideological terms like hacktivists, patriotic hacktivists, cyber terrorist, and cyber criminals, the very nature of the cyber domain obscures the actor's identity. Even if the actors were identified, their motivations would still be extremely difficult to know; so categorizing these threats without truly understanding the threat can potentially mislead defenders as they try to counter the threat. An article by Alexander Klimburg highlights a Russian perspective on the topic:

---

[34] Fletcher, *Aum Shinrikyo,* September 12, 2012

[35] Worried well is a term used to describe the psychologically affected who feel they are sick and seek out medical help but are actually physically well.

[36] Sayo Sasaki, "Aum Victim Keeps Memory Alive Via Film," *Japan Times on-Line,* http://www.japantimes.co.jp/text/nn20100309f1.html,(accessed March 9, 2010).

[37] Bob Woodward, *Obama's Wars,* 1st Simon & Schuster hardcover ed ed. (New York, N.Y.: Simon & Schuster, 2010), 10.

isolating cyberterrorism and cybercrime from the general context of international information security is, in a sense, artificial and unsupported ... it is primarily motivation that distinguishes acts of cyberterrorism, cybercrime, and military cyberattacks ... [without knowing the motivation one cannot] qualify what is going on as a criminal, terrorist or military political act.[38]

Some cyber threats have ideological motivations while others represent transnational organized crime. Cyber adversaries' motivations are murky at best.

This section will focus on actual cyber adversary capabilities and their associated potential threats to America; ignorantly trying to address attack motivations would mislead associated analysis. The author begins with acknowledging and highlighting some well-known cyber threats but then moves further to identify the larger direct cyber threats to Americans.

While WikiLeaks and Anonymous have regularly received headline news for their provocative actions, their direct risk to the American society is limited. Anonymous seeks an internet without any copyright restrictions; the group largely targets sanctioning bodies like the music recording industry and Hollywood cinema corporations. The group has elevated its attack targets by a recent distributed denial of service (DDOS) attack against the FBI's main websites after the FBI indicted members of leading file share sites MegaUpload and Pirate Bay. However, the FBI website was back on line and functioning within two hours. Prosecutors in the case are keeping a low profile in the case to avoid personal targeting.[39] Anonymous, as a group, does have the ability to disrupt some areas of American society but their history to date indicates little desire to attack America writ large (to disrupt the American way of life) or the typical American.

---

[38] Klimburg, "Mobilising Cyber Power," *Survival -London- International Institute for Strategic Studies* 53, no. 1 (February 2011), 1-2.

[39] Devlin Barrett, "Retaliation Fears Spur Anonymity in Internet Case," *Wall Street Journa-Eastern Edition* 59, no. 22, 3.

WikiLeaks seeks complete transparency of actions concerning governments and other globalized influential organizations. They recently posted over 250,000 U.S. Embassy cables for review by the world's populace. Since many of these cables were classified and identified U.S. informant names, lives were placed at risk.[40] So, while not a direct threat to the average American household, WikiLeaks does have an eroding effect upon the credibility and effectiveness American security by reducing its diplomatic ability to securely negotiate and communicate with other parties.

The larger cyber threat to typical Americans comes in the form of transnational criminal actors that can financially ruin households, businesses, and economy. Collectively, these cyber threats have created such a perceptive calamity that an industry of companies in the genre of LifeLock have emerged to protect individuals from the financial risks of that threat. Microsoft, Symantec, and McAfee form the first line of defense by screening viruses. However, the risk is not technical alone. Human actions play heavily into this domain. Phishing introduces lures through electronic elicitation to unwary targets who voluntarily divulge their personal information. This divulgence often results in the target's financial losses. One recent research effort recorded that while malware broadly cast into the internet retrieved a 5 percent success rate, smaller and more directed spear-phishing efforts that targets user interfaces received a nearly 65 percent success rate.[41]

Botnets results from the subordination of many disparate computers that can be harnessed together to create a significant computational resource that is easily directed

[40] Atika Schubert, "WikiLeaks Releases Entire Archive of U.S. Embassy Cables," *CNN World*, September 2, 2012.

[41] Mark Bowden, *Worm: The First Digital World War* (New York, N.Y.: Atlantic Monthly Press, 2011), 36.

against a target. Individual computer owners are often unaware that their computers are infected with malware that allows their computers to be leveraged by an outside hacker. Malware that affords this penetration is often easy to avoid if one is aware of how NSAs use their malware to infect computers. Botnet hackers regularly use the same phishing approaches noted above to gain information to build their botnets..

The key actors here are not of one single mindset but rather a loose band of similarly skilled individuals whose motivation ranges from revenge to profit. One threat example from within the U.S. attempted to use a logic bomb.

> …logic bombs can be massively destructive: in 2008, for example, a logic bomb planted by a disgruntled employee in the network of US mortgage giant Fannie Mae would have wiped out all 4,000 servers if it had been allowed to detonate."[42]

A foreign cyber threat exists as well. China alone has several million citizens working or studying computer sciences and information technology (IT) related fields. While the Chinese government suppresses political dissent and often uses the computer specialists of the People's Liberation Army (PLA) as its tool for this suppression, it understands the value of cyber warfare.[43] The CCP uses its citizens as part of its national security apparatus; it actually encourages its citizens to gain the skills for potential future use in national struggles. Much like Saudi Arabia cultivated Mujahedeen among its idle and troublesome citizens and then exported them to Afghanistan and Pakistan, China is cultivating cyber warriors and orienting them to targets outside its borders. There are

---

[42] Klimburg, 2.
[43] Qiao Liang and Wang Xiangsui, *Unrestricted Warfare* (Beijing: PLA Literature and Arts Publishing House Arts, 1999), 8.

actually Chinese government-sponsored hacking competitions where the government

posts the winners' awards.[44]

Ted Kaczynski (lone wolf)

Ted Kaczynski, also known as the UnaBomber, is an example of single individual

who caused over a decade of terror against leaders of America's technology enterprises.

The FBI describes him as a "twisted genius who aspires to be the perfect, anonymous

killer—who builds untraceable bombs and delivers them to random targets, who leaves

false clues to throw off authorities, who lives like a recluse…and tells no one of his secret

crimes."[45]

The Unabomber period in America was a unique time. For twenty years, a

mystery man with only a poorly drawn likeness randomly terrorized America. His

manifesto derided the techno-industrial sectors of the U.S.. In all, he killed three people

and injured another 26 in his sixteen separate attacks. His methods were simple; he built

then mailed or placed his bombs into destructive action.

The novel part of the Unabomber saga was that he was not a person from a

disadvantaged childhood nor did he have a limited education or intellect. Ted Kaczynski

was a very well educated man who possessed a Harvard degree, a PhD. in mathematics

from the University of Michigan, and taught at the University of California, Berkley.

This case illustrates that even a privileged and talented person can become ideologically

bent. Kaczynski self-radicalized, published a manifesto, and made himself an enduring

public threat. If a similar actor arose today, that person's heightened intellect and access

---

[44] Bowden, 116.
[45] Federal Bureau of Investigation, "FBI 100-the Unabomber," Department of Justice, https://www.fbi.gov/news/stories/2008/april/unabomber_042408 (accessed September 15, 2012).

to university laboratories could be a significant contributor in the context of current synthetic biology technologies threats.

Trans-National Criminal Organizations and their Attacks

Crime has always existed and is not a new concept to most people; criminals have even been used by the U.S. military to afford operational success. In World War II, New York's organized crime establishment was used to ferret out German spies/saboteurs in Port Elizabeth, and Lucky Luciano[46] facilitated an accommodation for Allied landings in Sicily.[47] Realizing that organized crime has abilities to support other disparate organizations should be established in national leadership's minds already. However, on October 11, 2011, many American's were surprised by Department of Justice indictments that tied together an American citizen, Hizballah, Iran, and Mexican drug cartels. An American citizen of Iranian descent, working with Hizballah operatives, was indicted in a murder for hire conspiracy against the Saudi Ambassador to the US.

> We should be concerned about a nexus between Iran, Hezbollah, and the drug cartels. This plot indicates a dangerous escalation of the Iranian government's role in the sponsorship of terrorism. Remember that World War I started because of an assassination of a foreign diplomat.[48]

The following section will discuss three transnational criminal organizations and highlight their capacities through their attacks. Drug trafficking organizations are one subset of TCOs. Understanding these organizations is essential to appreciate fully the

---

[46] Lucky Luciano was a notorious U.S. mobster with connections to organized crime in Sicily.
[47] T. J. English, Havana Nocturne: How the Mob Owned Cuba– and then Lost it to the Revolution (New York, N.Y.: William Morrow, 2008), 5.
[48] House Subcommittee on Counterterrorism and Intelligence, *Iranian Terror Operations on American Soil*, 112th Cong., 1st sess., 2011, 1.

"commodification" noted earlier in this thesis. The three TCOs discussed below are: Los Zetas, Colombian Revolutionary Armed Forces (FARC), and the Haqqani Network.

Los Zetas

The drug trafficking violence raging in Mexico has been headlines for a number of years. Warring drug trafficking organizations (DTOs) are battling over plazas or smuggling routes that move drugs from Latin and South America into the U.S. through its Southwest border. Over 47,000 murders have been documented since 2006, and many more undocumented ones are suspected. Mexican DTOs have increasingly branched out internationally, especially throughout the Western Hemisphere. With DTO revenues estimated at the $20-25 billion annually,[49] there is plenty of money available to buy capabilities, impunity, and operational reach that further DTO business ventures. Los Zetas are a leading DTO among the Mexican traffickers and their capabilities, shown through their rapid and brutal rise, will be discussed next.

The Los Zetas were initially hired as protection by the Gulf Cartel and were selected and recruited away from the Mexican Army's Special Forces. These soldiers were trained at Fort Benning's School of Americas by US, Israeli and French special forces professionals.[50] Their motivation for deserting the military was the overwhelming amount of money offered by the cartels compared to their military salaries. The Zetas held the position of the Gulf Cartel's enforcer for several years, and then they also ventured out into free-lancing for other DTOs. In 2010, they realized their potential and

---

[49] Congressional Research Service, *Mexico's Drug Trafficking Organizations Source and Scope of the Rising Violence: A Study Prepared Prepared for Members and Committees of Congress* by Congressional Research Service, August 2012 (Washington, D.C.: Government Printing Office, 2012), 39

[50] Albert De Amicis, *Los Zetas and La Familia Michoacana Drug Trafficking Organizations (DTOs)*, (Universityof Pittsburgh Press, 2010), 5.

began trafficking for themselves. Their break from the Gulf Cartel added yet another competitor for the drug plazas, and the resultant violence increased at even steeper rates.

Los Zetas operations have included a full range of operations from intimidation, kidnapping adversary's family members, killing media members, flamboyant tortures, mass executions, and platoon-sized military style operations. Combined with the specialized training both in the U.S. and Mexico, the Zetas also have the following weaponry and assets at their disposal: military grade rifles and machine guns, .50 Caliber machine guns, grenade launchers, surface to air missiles, explosives, up-armored vehicles, and helicopters.[51] The psychological effects from their tortures, executions, and kidnapping have helped to establish the Zetas as grim members of the DTO community that should not be challenged. The populace, many politicians, and government officials regularly yield way when matters involve the Zetas.

Los Zetas wisely use their notoriety in Mexico but drastically reduce it in the U.S.. Los Zetas have been credited with the mass murders of hundreds of people on the north side of the border across several occasions.[52] These killings target both Mexicans and immigrants inside rival DTO territory. Within the U.S., the Zetas use U.S. prison gangs to control U.S. street gangs who are their retail level of distribution. This outsourcing breaks the clear ties between them in their U.S. distribution system. This obfuscation also breaks any connected violence to them as well. Further, it stymies any potential U.S. outcry directly against them from the United States' "War on Drugs" – a twenty-year plus program that seemingly meanders on without any comprehensive plan of action and milestones to win.[53]

---

[51] Ibid,18.
[52] Sylvia Longmire, "Mexican DTO Influence Extends Deep into United States," *CTC Sentinal* 5, no. 7 (July 2012, 2012), 16.
[53] Ibid,17.

Los Zetas are positioned on the U.S. Southern border and have forward operating bases and organizational structures in a litany of U.S. cities.[54] One can readily see how this criminal organization has the potential to cause significant destruction and disruption within the U.S. should the violence in the south spill across the border into their retail level.

Colombian Revolutionary Armed Forces (FARC)

The FARC is an interesting threat group located in South America that has been on the U.S. Foreign Terrorist Organization list since 2002.[55] FARC began as an ideological insurgency that sought to replace the Colombian political system with one that was deeply socialist oriented. FARC's ideology soon merged with a Bolivarian revolution theme that well suited it to find affinity with the local lower economic classes. In pursuit of their goals, the FARC initially used extortion to provide a means to its revolutionary ways. Later, the group turned to narcotics trafficking as a supplement to its means. The rise of narcotics eventually dominated FARC's modus operandi and their political approaches became rigid and violent. These changes, along with reforms from the Colombian government, caused Colombia's populace to stop supporting the FARC.[56]

The FARC is novel today because it represents two relevant facts. First, it is effectively a defeated narco-insurgency within Colombia. Second, it is still a viable organization in the broader region and it operates with illicit criminal and terrorist actors. Venezuela is the strongest supporter of the FARC, but Ecuador and Nicaragua also have

[54] National Drug Intelligence Center, *National Drug Threat Assessment, 2011* (United States: US Dept of Justice, 2011), 13.

[55] Carlos A. Padilla, "The FARC and Hugo Chavez: Is Contemporary Venezuela a Threat to Colombia?" (Masters thesis, Naval Postgraduate School, 2010), 27.

[56] U.S. Army-Center for Army Lessons Learned, "Stability Operations in the Western Hemisphere: Observations, Insights, Lessons." Fort Leavenworth, KS.: Center for Army Lessons Learned (CALL), (May 2011), 45

histories of tacit approval.[57] The FARC can be expected to exist so long as its members have state sanctuaries. The benefit Venezuela receives back from supporting the FARC is discussed in the paragraphs below.

Venezuela is the primary supporter of the FARC and uses the group as a key exporter of the Bolivarian revolutionary ideology throughout Latin America. Hugo Chavez was Venezuela's leader until his death, and his ascendance was largely based upon Bolivarian ideology and corruption. Therefore, his platform and his future rely on the wellness of the ideology and his ability to maintain alliances with the proper political players in his country. Chavez leverages his FARC connections to afford him with needed narcotics monies to influence his political players while not being directly tied to its narcotic source.[58]

While the FARC has habitual relationships with Mexican DTOs as a key cocaine supplier,[59] the Venezuelan government affords the FARC access to sanctuary, weaponry, and access to other foreign and malign actors such as Iran and Hizballah. The U.S. Department of Homeland Security has reported that since the collusion between the FARC and Chavez' government began, a fivefold increase in suspicious flights out of Venezuela have occurred, as well as an accompanying tenfold increase in cocaine exports.[60]

---

[57] Padilla, 59-60

[58] Ibid, 89.

[59] Associated Press, "Colombia Rebels Linked to Mexico Drug Cartels," *New York Times*, http://www.nytimes.com/2008/10/08/world/americas/08mexico.html (accessed January 4, 2013).

[60] Ibid.

FARC regularly colludes with terrorists, and Margarita Island is an example nexus point for FARC and LH overlap.[61] Hizballah and FARC tie together from their sponsors' roots in oil production and OPEC memberships. Their operational-level ties ideologically link them at the Marxist level where they see the world divided between the oppressor and the oppressed. Both the FARC and LH view the U.S. as their common oppressor, and the cocaine revenues generated by U.S. dollars create a double pay-off in that cocaine undermines their U.S. adversary while empowering themselves. Training and military weapons exchanges are connections at these groups' tactical level. Anti-tank missiles, man portable air defense missiles, and asymmetric warfare training are the hallmark of the collusion. One novel and startling example of higher collusion is the sixty-six pound recovery of depleted uranium from FARC associates in the Bogotá suburbs.[62] Hizballah has also trained FARC fighters at its training camps inside of Lebanon.[63] Knowledge of LH tactics, techniques and procedures (TTPs) have now returned to Venezuela and are likely to migrate outwards from there among DTO relationships as FARC and Mexican DTOs intermingle. DTOs first used VBIEDs against Mexican first responders in 2011.[64]

---

[61] U.S. Army-Center for Army Lessons Learned, *Stability Operations in the Western Hemisphere: Observations, Insights, Lessons*,112.

[62] Joshua Goodman, "Colombia Probes FARC Ties to Uranium Seized in Bogota," , http://www.bloomberg.com/apps/news?pid=newsarchive&sid=a2kQfcdqP.ns (accessed September 30, 2012).

[63] Jon B. Perdue, *The War of all the People: The Nexus of Latin American Radicalism and Middle Eastern Terrorism* (Washington, D.C.: Potomac Books, 2012), 171.

[64] Scott Stewart, "The Perceived Car Bomb Threat in Mexico," STRATFOR, http://www.stratfor.com/weekly/20110413-perceived-car-bomb-threat-mexico (accessed October 29, 2012).

Haqqani Network (HQN)

The Haqqani Network is a militant group operating in the Eastern Afghanistan and the Karram Agency of Western Pakistan; it was designated a Foreign Terrorist Organization September 7, 2012.[65] HQN's origin dates back to the 1970s and has some linkages to the Central Intelligence Agency's (CIA) effort to create a guerilla force in Pakistan that would oppose Soviet efforts in Afghanistan. Today, HQN is among the leading U.S. adversaries in Afghanistan.[66] Further, it is sometimes a proxy force used by the Pakistan ISI to create a "near abroad" that isolates Islamabad from adversarial influences on both its Eastern and Western borders.

HQN opposes the Afghan government and NATO missions in Afghanistan because these entities erode its hard won influence in the region. The Heritage Foundation compiled HQN significant attacks to date as:

> Haqqani fighters were responsible for the storming of the Serena Hotel in Kabul during a high-level visit by Norwegian officials in January 2008; a suicide attack against the Indian embassy in Kabul in July 2008 that killed two senior Indian officials and over 50 others; a suicide attack on a CIA base in Khost Province in December 2009 that marked the most deadly attack on the CIA in 25 years; an attack on the U.S. Bagram Air Base in mid-May 2010; a multi-hour siege of the U.S. embassy in Kabul in September 2011; and a complex and coordinated attack on U.S. Base Camp Salerno in Khost Province on June 1, [2012].[67]

---

[65] U.S. Department of State, "Report to Congress on the Haqqani Network," US Government, http://www.state.gov/secretary/rm/2012/09/197474.htm (accessed September 20, 2012).

[66] Ashley Frantz, "The Haqqani Network, a family and a terror group," www.cnn.com/2012/09/07/world/who-is-haqqani/index.html (accessed January4, 2013).

[67] House Committee on Foreign Affairs, Subcommittee, *Hearings on Combating the Haqqani Terrorist Network*, 112th Cong., 2nd Sess., 2012, 4.

The U.S. Ambassador refers to HQN as "the worst of the worst...a group of killers, pure and simple." And it has been attributed with responsibility for approximately15 percent of the U.S.' casualties in the Afghanistan Theater.[68]

HQN is notable because it is tied to the Taliban and specifically with the Quetta Shura,[69] but its members are not primarily Islamic in their motivations. The strongest capability that HQN possesses is its breadth of international activity and business involvement, both licit and illicit, throughout the region as well as the Persian Gulf. The organization is financially established much like DTOs and TCOs throughout the world. One New York Times analyst and regional expert calls this group the "Sopranos of Afghanistan."[70]

Much like any criminal organization, HQN profits from the instability found in the Afghanistan-Pakistan border region. Where the state is weak, other powers fill that vacuum, and HQN has easily dominated this region until recently. Much like the warlords before them, HQN makes profits both from the war and for the war. Unlike the warlords before them, they are able to co-opt an Islamic ideological message to increase revenues from sympathetic donors overseas and inspire zealots to extreme actions.

Finally, HQN has been building its networks and influence for over thirty years and has diversified broadly and widely. These resources have been used to support numerous Islamic militant groups over the years, including AQ. Its reach can be seen through its numerous training camps located in North Waziristan. Although no direct open source linkages have connected Faisal Shahzad's May 1, 2010 attempted Times

---

[68] Ibid,4.

[69] The Quetta Shura is a conglomerate of al-Qaeda senior leaders and members of the Taliban that fled from Afghanistan into Quetta, Pakistan to escape U.S./ISAF attacks.

[70] Mark Mazzetti, Shane Scott, and Alissa Rubin, "Brutal Haqqani Crime Clan Bedevils U.S. in Afghanistan," *New York Times*, September 24, 2011.

Square car bombing to HQN, U.S. law enforcement officials have released that he was trained before the attack in HQN dominated territory.[71] One can infer that the attack was retribution for increased U.S. targeting of HQN in Afghanistan.

While all NSAs are capable of threating to the U.S., most are not intent upon that end. The nature of NSAs is that they each seek to further their own goals and purposes. Those NSAs without malicious intent but with capacity to market can ultimately be just as dangerous as the NSAs with intent. Attriting the NSA capacity can be just as important as the intent and balancing these two goals is likely beyond the scope of just the Department of Homeland Security.

---

[71] Mark Mazzetti and Shane Scott, "Evidence Mounts for Taliban Role in Bomb Plot," *New York Times*, May 5, 2010.

CHAPTER 4: POTENTIAL IMPACTS TO AMERICAN SOCIETY

Non-state adversaries have used destruction, disruption, and psychological attacks on America. Destruction refers to the permanent removal of a highly-valued person, place, or thing from its normal use. Disruption is the turbulence that places the American way of life out of balance; normalcy is attrited, and adaption and innovation are required to recover and return to a normal state. Psychological effects address the possible fears arising from destruction and disruption attacks. At times, psychological attacks are possible even when no actual attack or disruption have occurred. Finally, psychological fears can create greater disruption to a society than an actual attack. These three attack methods will be discussed in greater detail below.

Destruction

Destruction is an adversarial non-state threat actor (NSA) attack method that refers to the ruining or removal of a high-valued asset from America's normal use or reliance. This type of assault has been the NSA's most direct and most used attack method. Typical American high value targets include people, symbolic assets, and critical infrastructure; however, the American way of life is also a prime psychological target of U.S. adversaries. America's attackers come from a broad range of motivations and that threat diversity makes mitigating them all the harder. These destruction threats are discussed below in greater detail.

Killing

The act of killing Americans is a destruction method that has been consistently used by U.S. adversaries. Overseas examples include the bombing of the Marine Corps barracks in Beirut and Khobar Towers that killed 241 and 16 U.S. service members stationed in Lebanon and Saudi Arabia, respectively.[1] While these murders have been clearly linked to Islamic terrorists, other widely public murders of American citizens also display the threat realities of modern non-state actors at home.

In 2002, John Muhammed and Lee Boyd Malvo formed a murderous team that became known as "the D.C. Sniper." These two used commercially available firearms and a modified car to terrorize Americans in random slayings along the I-95 corridor from Montgomery County, Maryland to Ashland, Virginia. In all, three weeks of mayhem resulted in ten Americans dead and three more critically wounded. Like the TCO violence noted in Chapter 3, John Mohammed's motivation was plain criminality instead of ideological motivations. Muhammed's reason for killing so many has been widely reported as a method to blur his connections to his ex-wife's murder.[2]

These murders and their timing held the broader Capital region captive for weeks and psychologically affected many more. During this period, headline news regularly declared yet another new victim time and again. The randomness of the killings and the wide-range of venues induced a feeling of uneasiness across a region. In a survey taken after the attacks, nearly half the respondents (45 percent) said that during the attack period they chose to alter their plans and to venture out only if the trip was necessary.[3]

---

[1] John J. Ziegler and Air University (U.S.). Air Command and Staff College., *From Beirut to Khobar Towers: Improving the Combating Terrorism Program* (Maxwell Air Force Base, AL.: Air Command and Staff College, 1998), 6.

[2] Jack Censer and William Miller, *On the Trail of the D.C. Sniper: Fear and the Media* (Charlottesville, VA: University of Virginia Press, 2010), 17.

[3] Jeffrey Schulden et al., "Psychological Responses to the Sniper Attacks: Washington D.C. Area, October 2002," *American Journal of Preventive Medicine* 31, no. 4 (October 2006), 324.

That self sequestration reflected a significant societal shift in behavior; this shift was created by just two people empowered with easily available capabilities.[4]

Another example of killings can be found in the psychopathic murders at Columbine High School, Colorado, April 20, 1999. Two students, Eric Harris—who was clinically diagnosed with psychopathic traits—and Dylan Kliebold—his manic-depressed under study—planned and executed a killing spree that shocked a nation. These two field-tested firearms and homemade explosives with the full intent of killing as many people as possible in a bombing attack of their high school. They studied student daily activities and determined peak occupancy times of their kill box, the school cafeteria. Their attacks were launched with minute level of accuracy. Anticipated first responders were targeted outside the school at two ingress points with car bombs. Inside the school, smaller explosive devices were built and employed to herd students into the cafeteria where larger explosives would drop the ceiling from the library above onto the students and faculty with the intention to kill all present.[5]

The plan went awry when the main bombs failed to detonate as planned and the attack turned into an "active shooter"[6] spree instead of the intended bombings. Harris and Kliebold shot 33 students and faculty; twelve were killed and 21 injured before the attackers killed themselves. The killers were dead for nearly two hours before first responders entered the building to "de-escalate" the situation.[7]

---

[4] John W. Kiser, "Terrorism and our Domestic Peril," The Eisenhower Institute, http://www.eisenhowerinstitute.org/publications/archives/2002/Kiser_terrorism.dot (accessed Sept 18, 2012).

[5] David Cullen, *Columbine*, 1st ed. (New York, N.Y.: Grand Central Publishing, 2009), 432.

[6] DHS defines an Active Shooter as, "…an individual actively engaged in killing or attempting to kill people in a confined and populated area; in most cases, active shooters use firearms(s) and there is no pattern or method to their selection of victims."

[7] Cullen, 13.

Critical Infrastructure and Symbolic Assets

Non-state actors have regularly focused on symbolic targets to maximize their attack's affect upon the targeted populace. LH attacked the United States' Marine Corps barracks and the U.S. Embassy in Beirut and received an American military withdrawal for its audacity. Al Qaeda progressed through its learning curve by first attacking embassies, then military targets, and finally achieved their much-desired response by attacking the U.S. homeland. Chechen rebels understood their target audience better and achieved maximum effect by seizing an entire grade school in Beslan. The attack resulted in all terrorists killed but also 187 children dead.[8] The World Trade Centers were key symbols of the United States' business community and possibly also the world's business center when attacked on 9/11. The economic impact alone had a far-reaching effect, as markets dropped nearly 14 percent on the week and remained lower in value for nearly a year[9] (see Figure 2). Additionally, with nearly 3000 people from numerous nations killed that morning, the broad psychological impact had an amplifying consequence on the overall impact of this single terrorist event.

---

[8] John Dunlop, "The September 2004 Beslan Terrorist Incident-New Findings," *Center on Democracy, Development, and the Rule of Law Working Papers*, no. 115 (July, 2009), 3.

[9] Cengage Learning, "The Economic Impact of 9/11," Gale World Headquarters, http://behindtheheadlines.info/teaching911/the-economic-impact-of-911-interactive-chart-dow-jones-industrial-average.php (accessed November 10, 2012).

Photo Removed Due to Copyright Restrictions

Figure 2-The Economic Impact of 9/11[10]

Disruption

Just-in-Time Society

The American way of life relies upon ready access to demanded goods and services. The pace of these transactions has greatly increased from even a decade ago. The "invisible hand" of the free market drives businesses to ever more efficiency as businesses pursue their maximum profit levels, and this often means minimizing their overhead by reducing their stockage levels.[11] Just-in-time supply is a concept that allows the consumer to receive the demanded product and/or service without requiring the service provider to store the good in his warehouses any longer than necessary. This reduced storage decreases the amount of the seller's capital associated outside of direct transactions. While this stockage approach increases profits and reduces local storage

---

[10] Ibid.

[11] Adam Smith and Edwin Cannan, *The Wealth of Nations* (New York: Modern Library, 2000), 16.

requirements, it also reduces the ability for the supplier to respond effectively to unforeseen demand surges in his product/services.

During hurricane season, Americans regularly make runs on grocery stores and gas stations to hoard items for near term possible needs. Often they purchase more than the situation requires. These shoppers leave grocery marts' shelves bare well beyond the typical eggs, milk and bread staples. These runs leave much of the populace without any supplies to purchase.[12] Grocers run their just-in-time supply chain on an approximate two-day shelf-life cycle, relying heavily on the just-in-time resupply to meet customer demand. When demand spikes, there are not adequate surge capacities within the stores to compensate for the hoarding. Ultimately, numerous Americans are left without their essentials if those items are not already stocked at residences.

Perhaps a viral/biological epidemic best illustrates the unintended consequences and detrimental nature of the just-in-time society paired with the public's tendency to hoard essentials. Emergency vaccine distribution plans such as Florida's plan allow the "head of household" to draw medicine for up to 15 other family members. Similar plans are particularly susceptible to failure because some will draw and hold much more than they need thereby denying others from the finite supplies.[13] Additionally, one can expect full distribution efforts to fail due to other factors such as: self-sequestration driven by fear, accessibility limitation from destroyed infrastructure, and simple ignorance of the timely information needed to complete the distribution.

---

[12] Gregory Gilligan, "Looming Storm Prompts a Run on Grocery Stores," *Richmond Times-Dispatch*, January 16, 2013.

[13] Daniel Walsh and Chuck VanGronigen, "Logistics Modeling: Improving Resource Management and Public Information Strategies in Florida," *Journal of Business Continuity & Emergency Planning* 5, no. 3 (October 11, 2011), 4.

Cascading Failures

The Department of Energy's Idaho National Labs hosted a table top forum in

2008 with leading industry and regional leaders to discuss the interconnectedness of

disparate businesses within their operations. This exercise sought to examine what the

impacts of one business sector might have on associated sectors. This idea of a ripple

effect has come to be better known as cascading effect and addresses second, third and

further effects emanating from an initial stimulus within a common system.[14]

To test the theory, the lab aggregated each of the business leaders and local utility

service providers into the business sectors of: agriculture/food, water, energy,

transportation, communication, and finance. Within each business sector, testers then

surveyed and charted how each business directly interacted with each other. A scenario

was posed to the leaders to examine what impact absenteeism would have on their

business if 25 percent of their workers did not come into work for six to eight weeks. A

25 percent absenteeism rate for four to eight weeks has been researched and determined

as a conservative estimate in cases of pandemics.[15] The qualitative responses ranged

from green for no impact, yellow for moderate impact, red for significant impact and

black for catastrophic impact. Key reasons for absenteeism include the immediately ill,

caregivers to those who are ill, and those psychologically effected who simply fear

contracting the illness from others. Historical pandemics have lasted for many weeks

across numerous cities. Figure 3 illustrates that the 1918 influenza epidemic dwelled

within the American populace for nearly two months before burning itself out.

---

[14] Eric Allely, M.D. *National Response to Biologic Contagion: Lessons from Pandemic Planning* (Suffolk, VA: Joint Center for Operational Analysis, 2008), 47.
[15] A. Lesperance and J. Miller, Preventing Absenteeism and Promoting Resilience among Health Care Workers in Biological Emergencies (Washington, D.C.;. Dept. of Energy, 2009), 15-16.

Quarantine was a key mitigation tool used in the 1918 epidemic. With today's increased

connectedness, duration and destruction could be even greater.

Photo Removed Due to Copyright Restrictions

Figure 3-The Long Duration of the 1918 Spanish Flu Epidemic[16]

Within each business sector survey, individual responses showed that respective

businesses would be degraded and that associated output would be reduced but that their

business would continue. When the sector business leaders were then asked what impact

the reduced output of associated businesses would have on their own business, the sector

leaders generally increased their impact to a significant impact instead of just moderate.

---

[16] Howard Markel, Harvey Lipman, and J. Alexander Navarro, "Nonpharmaceutical Interventions Implemented by US Cities during the 1918-1919 Influenza Pandemic," *Journal of American Medicine* 298, no. 6 (August 8, 2007), 644.

Business owners realized they heavily relied on other businesses' timely output to support their own operations.[17]

Re-assembling all of the sectors together again, the facilitators showed the linkage charts between sectors illustrating how finance related to energy and energy to transportation, among many other connections. The question was then asked, "What impact would the degraded sectors supporting their particular sectors have on their businesses?" General system deterioration was reflected across all sectors. Sectors reflecting merely moderate impacts become exceptional as most sectors reflected significant impacts. The key insight taken away was that the transportation sectors went nearly completely "black." The transportation sector realized catastrophic impact.[18]

In a just in time economy/society, the transportation system is essential. Within the U.S., products largely live in the transportation pipeline instead of warehouses. Without a well-functioning transportation sector, products and services stop and both the end user and the supplier wither. The scenario above illustrates how simple disruption of human activity can have detrimental cascading effects on the American way of life.

Second-Order Effects

Second-order effects are worth discussing because they have potential to over shadow the initial crisis-causing event. Second order effect impacts to supply and demand were discussed earlier in the chapter, and while these disruptions are inconvenient phenomena, they generally do not become critical when the adversary is inclement weather. The majority of weather events generally pass with limited duration and lasting impact. However, when catastrophic weather events create dire or more

---

[17] Eric Allely, 49.
[18] Ibid, 49.

persistent situations, those must be studied to address ways to mitigate and minimize the effects in future occurrences. This section will address unanticipated second order effects recently seen during Hurricane Katrina disaster response operations.

During crisis events, the demand for first responders increases dramatically. What has been observed in recent natural-disaster crisis events is that during a crisis period, the availability of essential first responders actually drops compared to non-crisis periods. The graphic in Figure 5 is from the Joint Center for Operational Analysis' Katrina Study displays this reality concisely. The red-hashed area represents the unmet requirement of government emergency workers over time.

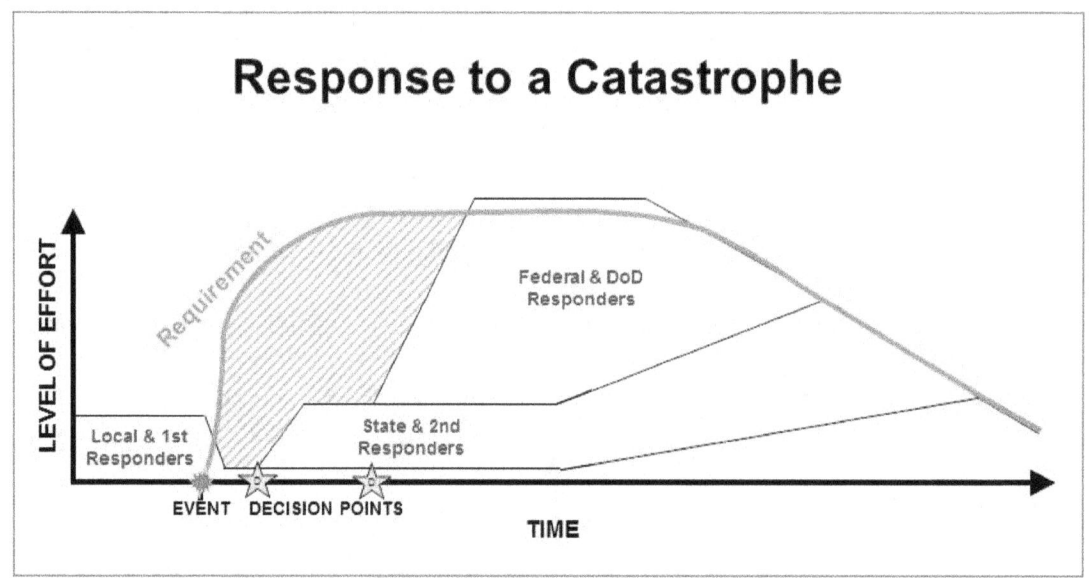

Figure 5-Emergency Responder Availability during Times of Crisis[19]

The reason for this unfortunate reality is often two fold. First, during times of crises first responders may not have the capacity to report to work due to transportation limitations. Road washouts, flooded vehicles, and/or fire damages can limit the willing responder to report for duty. Second, the first responder may not be willing to report for

[19] Gregory Gecowets and Jefferson Marquis, "Applying the Lessons of Hurricane Katrina," *Joint Forces Quarterly* 48 (First Quarter, 2008), 72.

duty and public service because they have personal pressing concerns they must manage

before they can support the broader public.[20] Two examples below address the second

condition and highlight a critical concern in emergency planning matters.

> When participants [firefighters and EMS] were asked if they would report
> to work despite having sick family members at home, who were ill … 70.4
> % responded they would remain home and not report for duty[21]

> Qureshi et al. (2005) surveyed New York healthcare workers about their
> willingness to report to work during a chemical event, a smallpox
> epidemic, a radiation event, and a SARS epidemic—67.7 % said they
> would be willing to report to work for a chemical event, compared with
> 61.1 % for smallpox, 57.3 % for radiation, and 48.4 % for SARS.[22]

When the majority of first responders are absent during the crisis period then the

crisis period can be expected to extend for a longer duration and the magnitude of small

problems can multiply. Based on the Hurricane Katrina experience (see Figure 5) and the

two surveys above, the populace can be expected to endure greater suffering during initial

stages of the crisis when their primary means of recovery relies heavily on external

entities such as first responders and associated government-oriented solutions.

Psychological Impacts

The previous section addressed how disruption effects can cause cascading

failures with the American society. The psyche of the terrorist's targeted populace is

often just as important as the destruction of any given article associated with an attack.

As has been illustrated for several millennia among wise warriors such as Sun Tzu, "The

---

[20] Lesperance and Miller, 2-6.
[21] David V. Johnson, "Assessing the Impact of Employee Absenteeism on Emergency Operations during a Pandemic" (Masters, National Fire Academy, 2008), 17.
[22] Lesperance and Miller, 15.

supreme art of war is to subdue the enemy without fighting."[23] An opponent who has

been mentally defeated and/or refuses to fight has ceded the war to the aggressor

Popular Will

In the 1990s, Al Qaeda made several attacks against America but these early

attacks never quite achieved the response they sought. AQ attempted to affect the U.S.

popular will and stop U.S. influence projection into historically "Islamic Lands." Using

the "DIME"[24] lens to view AQ's attack on U.S. sources of influence, it attacked the

military when it attacked the USS Cole. Against information/new ideas, AQ used fatwas,

sermons, and the internet radicalization efforts to counter the western cultural influences

that inspired much of its reason for being. AQ attacked U.S. embassies in Kenya and

Tanzania to counter America's diplomatic means, but all three of these attacks failed to

gain much response from the U.S. populace or changes to U.S. policy. With the 9/11

attack, AQ ultimately attempted to defeat the U.S. by attacking the U.S. psyche through

an attack within the homeland against the economic system that had direct linkages to all

Americans. While the group caused turbulence in the economic system, that system

eventually recovered. AQ was more successful in attacking the U.S. psyche; 9/11

certainly got American's attention.[25]

Americans generally felt vulnerable for the first time in decades; "everything has

changed" was an oft-heard expression in America shortly after the attacks on 9/11. U.S.

---

[23] Sun Tsu, *The Art of War*, trans. J. J. L. Duyvendak and Hanzhang Tao, Penguin Classics Deluxe Edition ed. (London, U.K.: Wordsworth, 1998), 384.
[24] DIME is a commonly used term used to describe the U.S. instruments of power. The acronym stands for diplomatic, information, military and economic means used to positively influence the international environment toward U.S. national goals.
[25] Shelley McCardle and H. Rosoff, The Dynamics of Evolving Beliefs, Concerns Emotions, and Behavioral Avoidance Following 9/11: A Longitudinal Analysis of Representative Archival Samples (Boston, MA: National Institute of Health, 2012), 2.

national will was not broken; instead, similar to London's populace after German bombing campaigns, the American people were more steeled as a society than before. Revenge and retribution was the typical reaction. However, on the individual level, Americans did feel more vulnerable.[26]

Previous discussion on threat actors and attacks in Chapters 2 and 3 illustrate how the psychological effects on individual choices and attitudes can lead to the detriment of broader society. In the Tokyo sarin attacks, the "worried well"[27] saturated the health care systems and denied service to those who really did need medical attention. Fears in pandemics or perceived pandemics can lead to worker absenteeism that can cripple the just-in-time economy and modern way of life.

Mental Resilience

Mental resilience, the psychological ability to bounce back after a catastrophe, is essential for American recovery following a disaster. According to the Journal of Consulting and Clinical Psychology, resilience is greatly attrited by both available resources and social networks. [28] So, as Americans become more independent and less familial (less tribal) they decrease in their opportunities for resilience. Further, as Americans become more accustomed to living a life style of convenience in a just-in-time approach, the quantity of their stored resources is also reduced. Both situations lend typical Americans to be less prepared for the mental resiliency needed to absorb attacks or natural catastrophes.

---

[26] Dinesh Bhugra, "9/11: Mental Health in the Wake of Terrorist Attacks," *International Review of Psychiatry* 22, no. 2 (April 2010), 224.

[27] "Worried-Well" refers to healthy persons who seek medical attention when there is no need for medical care, the term often is related to psychological trauma resulting from attacks and natural disasters.

[28] Stevan E. Hobfoll et al., "Trajectories of Resilience, Resistance, and Distress during Ongoing Terrorism: The Case of Jews and Arabs in Israel," *Journal of Consulting & Clinical Psychology* 77, no. 1 (February 2009), 138.

The chart in Figure 4 displays human responses to a traumatic event or for purposes of this thesis, an NSA attack. The goals for American society should be to reduce risks of being attacked and also to reduce the psychological impacts of attacks should they occur. The Y axis represents one's response intensity to an attack and the X axis displays one's remaining psychological distress after the attack. The black boxes represent initial stimulus or NSA attack. Block (a) located on the X-axis represents a single attack without direct impact on the target/populace while block (b) represents an attack with direct impact. Note the differences in realized intensity or psychological trauma when a directly impacting attack occurs. Block (a) might be a story about an attack on others and block (b) would be an attack on you or someone close to you. In block (c), reaction is desirable but recovery from the attack is too slow. This block shows an awareness to a threat type but an unpreparedness to deal with it. Block (d), habituation, shows reduced reaction and quick recovery times to direct impact attacks. Habituation response should be the goal when pursuing mental resilience. Habituation is best accomplished when the person realizes a potential hazard, has considered appropriate responses, and is prepared for the event. Citizen response during the bombing of London is an example of habituation. In block (e), a direct attack spikes the person's psychological responses. While the subject may reasonably recover from these attacks, they are mentally unprepared for recurrence.

A well-informed and prepared populace is essential to attain a desired habituation response reflected in block (d). Understanding the potential threats help one acclimatize to the threat risk and even prepare to mitigate them. Ignorance of the threats results in surprise when attacks occur. Surprise increases mental trauma and extends the recovery time back to normalcy. Multiple surprise attacks can be psychologically devastating. The anthrax and D.C. sniper attacks that followed shortly after 9/11 exacerbated the psychological stress felt in America.

Photo Removed Due to Copyright Restrictions

Figure 4-Societies Responses to Negative Events[29]

---

[29] Bruce Michael Bongar, *Psychology of Terrorism* (New York, N.Y.: Oxford University Press, 2007), 49.

CHAPTER 5: U.S. APPROACHES TO COUNTER NON-STATE ACTORS THREATS

This chapter examines the U.S. government's approaches to achieve Homeland Security goals. National policies explicitly state that non-state actors are a threat to the homeland and that Department of Homeland Security (DHS) has lead agency responsibility for securing the homeland. The author lays out national approaches to countering non-state actor threats and discusses gaps found in these approaches.

Policies Establishing National Goals for Homeland Security

After the attacks of 9/11, an increased focus was placed upon protection of the U.S. homeland. The consistent government approach to protection has been top-down where the federal government strives to reach down and coordinate with local municipalities. The 2012 Defense Strategic Guidance (DSG) better acknowledges the realities that the homeland is also an operating environment and recognizes the increasing potential for America to face another attack or natural disaster.[1] The federal government is proactively addressing the reality that a complete success in deterring all attacks and catastrophes in the homeland is unlikely. The Bipartisan Policy Committee Report card on the 9/11 10th Anniversary states, "Our terrorist adversaries and the tactics and techniques they employ are evolving rapidly. We will see new attempts, and likely successful attacks."[2]

The concept of resilience has taken hold under the Obama administration and this administration refers to the concept over 25 times within its 2010 National Security

---

[1] Office of the Secretary of Defense, *Sustaining U.S. Global Leadership: Priorities for 21st Century Defense by Leon Panetta.* (Washington, D.C.: Government Printing Office, 2012), 4.

[2] Lee Hamilton and Thomas Kean, *Tenth Anniversary Report Card the Status of the 9/11 Commission Recommendations* (Washington, D.C.: Bipartisan Policy Center, 2011), 1.

Strategy (NSS)[3] and Presidential Policy Decision (PPD)-8[4]. The focus on resiliency shows an environmental understanding that extends beyond just interdicting potential attackers. These two documents acknowledge that resiliency includes the ability to deter, and should deterrence fail, absorb and rebound after an attack.

Presidential Policy Directive-8 (PPD-8): National Preparedness

PPD-8 established in writing "The National Preparedness Goal[5]" as a tasker for DHS Secretary Napolitano. The National Preparedness Goal identified relevant threats and established Homeland "preparedness" objectives; DHS used this document to align its efforts in support of the NSS. The Homeland Security Strategic Plan 2011 is the linkage between National Security direction and DHS approaches to achieve security and resiliency in America. The five DHS mission areas from these policy directions are discussed in the DHS Strategic Plan section below.

National Preparedness Goal

The National Preparedness Goal's mission statement is: "A secure and resilient Nation with the capabilities required across the whole community to prevent, protect against, mitigate, respond to, and recover from the threats and hazards that pose the greatest risk."[6] Lines of effort are based upon a risk assessment that examines the

---

[3] U.S. President, *National Security Strategy* (Washington, D.C.: Government Printing Office, May 2010) 3-60.

[4] U.S. President, *Presidential Policy Directive/PPD-8: National Preparedness* (Washington D.C.: Government Printing Office, March 2011), 1-6.

[5] The National Preparedness Goal is a policy document directed by PPD-8 that identified the nations largest threats and approaches to the identified threats. Resiliency is identified as a key goal to mitigate the nations's risks.

[6] U.S. Department of Homeland Security, *National Preparedness Goal* (Washington, D.C.: Government Printing Office, 2011), 26.

contemporary environment facing the nation; that assessment clearly acknowledges the U.S. now faces broader threats than simply countering adversarial nation states.

DHS Strategic Plan for Fiscal Years 2012-2016

The DHS has executive agency responsibilities for homeland security. DHS' strategic plan states, "…Our [DHS] duties are wide-ranging, our goal is clear: a safe, secure, and resilient America."[7] With guidance from the NSS, PPD-8 and the National Preparedness Goal, DHS developed their department's strategic plan. DHS uses five mission areas or lines of effort in support of the National Preparedness Goal:

Mission 1: Preventing Terrorism and Enhancing Security

Mission 2: Securing and Managing Our Borders

Mission 3: Enforcing and Administering Our Immigration Laws

Mission 4: Safeguarding and Securing Cyberspace

Mission 5: Ensuring Resilience to Disasters

The non-state actor threats (NSA) highlighted in earlier chapters cut across DHS' five mission areas. While DHS is working and learning how to protect the U.S. homeland, gaps remain in the current approach.

DHS Mission Gaps

This section discusses the DHS mission areas, agencies charged with leading that mission, and some of the risks remaining in current approaches. This section also discusses some threats posed by NSAs that are outside of current DHS approaches.

---

[7] U.S. Department of Homeland Security, *Department of Homeland Security Strategic Plan Feb 2012* (Washington, D.C.: Government Printing Office, 2012), 41.

Mission 1: Preventing Terrorism and Enhancing Security

Mission 1 is to protect America from terrorist attacks regardless of terrorist group or attack method, but this mission is exclusively managed by the Transportation Security Agency (TSA). TSA is the DHS' sole action arm within the mission but this agency is only focused on air travel related threats. Coordination with the Department of Justice and USNORTHCOM are not even broached within the current DHS approach, much less tracked and validated for adequacy. In the current environment, terrorist ingress routes outside of established air ports of entry (POEs) are also outside DHS measuring and tracking. The DHS focus at land POEs is primarily illegal aliens and not terrorists.

The Domestic Nuclear Detection Office (DNDO)[8] monitors the sea and rail lines of communication for radiological threats that may be imported through commercial containers. While DNDO's efforts are certainly worthwhile, they only address radiological threats like fissile materials, radiological dispersal devices (RDDs), and smuggled nuclear weapons. The acceptable threshold of containers inspected is listed as FOUO and not readily available but what they are not screening for is clear. DHS is not screening sea ports of entry for terrorists. Even though TSA is earnestly enforcing immigration at the land and air POEs, what is clearly absent from measure is the checking of vessels and ships for potential threat actors aboard them. Although illegal aliens from Latin and South America largely arrive via foot,[9] Pacific-based illegal aliens often arrive by ship similar to LeT's attack described earlier. DHS enforces the screening process of travelers using the legal process, but it fails to measure illegal entrants arriving

---

[8] DNDO is a DHS managed agency whose primary mission is the detection of nuclear and fissile materials within the U.S.

[9] Ananda Rose, "Death in the Desert," *New York Times*, June 22, 2012.

by sea. Further, the Department has reduced its enforcement of illegals arriving by foot.[10] Pedestrian illegal entrants will be discussed further below.

Mission 2: Securing and Managing Our Borders

This mission area protects the U.S. borders from illegal penetration of persons, narcotics and other contraband items. The Southern border of the United States is currently the area of most risk because human trafficking and narcotics generally flow from the South and Central America through Mexico into the U.S.. The U.S. Customs and Border Patrol (CBP) is responsible for Mission 2, but far too few CBP officers exist to actually secure the full border.[11] CBP's primary effort is securing the ports of embarkation (POEs) and complements that effort by using roving intercept teams that bolster POE operations. However, their capacity is too small to cover the entire 1933 miles of border length.

The border mission's manpower shortfall might be best illustrated by the 2010 mobilization of 1,200 U.S. Army National Guardsmen to bolster border security.[12] Another example of this insecurity is illustrated by the Bureau of Land Management (BLM, an agency managed outside of DHS by the U.S. Department of Interior) that recently posted numerous signs 100 miles north of the U.S.'s southern border warning American travelers that "...the area is unsafe because of drug and alien smugglers."[13] This area covers nearly 60 miles of the U.S. border and Sheriff Joe Arpaio of Arizona

---

[10] U.S. Department of Homeland Security, *U.S. Department of Homeland Security Annual Performance Report* (Washington D.C.: US Government Printing Office, 2011), 62

[11] Army National Guard-Stand to Magazine, "Army National Guard Operation Phalanx," United States Army, http://www.army.mil/article/56819/Army_National_Guard_Operation_Phalanx/ (accessed January 17, 2013).

[12] Ibid, 1

[13] Jerry Seper and Matthew Cella, "Signs in Arizona Warn of Smuggler Dangers," *Washington Times*, August 31, 2010, 2.

claims that DTOs functionally control these areas of the U.S..[14] One could call parts of the U.S. border functionally ungoverned, or unsecured.

DTOs and LH regularly run human trafficking operations that penetrate the inadequately secured U.S. borders. These smuggling operations extend deep into the U.S. and completely bypass DHS inspectors working U.S. POEs. DHS is aware of this problem and its volume, so much so that these particular ingressors have their own term of art, "special interest aliens."[15] Merely tightening control at U.S. POEs has little constraining effect on adversaries who can simply enter the U.S. via uncontrolled areas described by the BLM that are away from the well managed POEs. One can see there is a clear disconnect between national level goals and the actual ability to secure the border from illicit actors that regularly cross into the United States.

Freedom of access into the U.S. has led to DTOs establishing operations in over one-thousand U.S. cities. This increase is nearly fourfold since 2009.[16] The government has repeatedly stated that the risk to drug violence spillover is low. However, this statement is quite narrow in scope because DHS defines "spillover violence" as:

> …deliberate, planned attacks by the cartels on U.S. assets, including civilian, military, or law enforcement officials, innocent U.S. citizens, or physical institutions such as government buildings, consulates, or businesses. This definition does not include trafficker on trafficker violence, whether perpetrated in Mexico or the U.S.[17]

---

[14] Joe Arpaio and Len Sherman, *Joe's Law: America's Toughest Sheriff Takes on Illegal Immigration, Drugs, and Everything Else that Threatens America* (New York, N.Y.: AMACOM, 2008), 79.

[15] Special Interests Aliens refers to illegal aliens entering into the U.S. from countries that possess active organizations (AQ, Hizballah, Al-Shabaab among others) to the U.S.

[16] National Drug Intelligence Center, *National Drug Threat Assessment, 2011*, U.S. Department of Justice (Washington, D.C. August 2011), 13.

[17] Congressional Research Service, *Southwest Border Violence Issues in Identifying and Measuring Spillover Violence A Study Prepared Prepared for Members and Committees of Congress* by Congressional Research Service, June 2011 (Washington, D.C.: Government Printing Office, 2011), 16.

The "...deliberate, planned" part of the definition only measures a pre-planned and intentional act of violence against the U.S.. This definition skews the nature of spillover violence by requiring intent instead of result. Further distorting the realities of this violence, DHS also states that violence among drug traffickers in the U.S. does not constitute spillover violence either. The violence in Mexico is often between traffickers but also claims numerous innocent lives during the battles. One can see how this narrowly scoped definition falls short of accurately measuring DTO violence within U.S. borders.

Texas defines spillover violence as, "Mexican cartel related violence that occurs in Texas. We include aggravated assault, extortion, kidnapping, torture, rape, and murder."[18] Using this broader definition, one can now cite realistic DTO related activities in America.

Violence related to DTOs is regularly occurring in the US.[19] Whether these violent-DTO related acts are pre-planned is irrelevant to the affected Americans. DHS' mission of "enhancing security" is failing along the borders and, as seen in DTO proliferation into U.S. cities, DTOs do not just remain along the borders. Some examples of the violence within U.S. borders include beheadings, kidnappings, extortion, and multiple-homicide slayings. "Sicaros" are drug traffickers' hit men who assassinate as well as torture and have been linked to Los Zeta operatives working in the U.S.[20] Local

---

[18] Ibid.
[19] Arpaio and Sherman, 248
[20] Tony Mena, "Mexico: Our Next AOR?" *The Foreign Affairs Officers Journal* XIV, no. 2 (May 2011), 10.

law enforcement officials along the border have been the most vocal about these threats while Federal officials decline to associate locally highlighted violence with spill over.[21]

Mission 3: Enforcing and Administering Our Immigration Laws

Immigration and Customs Enforcement (ICE) primarily leads this DHS mission area that ensures illegal aliens do not remain in the U.S.. DHS measures its performance at POEs and is satisfied that adversary threats are not coming through them, but deportation is focused on just crime-related illegals not the crime of illegally migrating itself. Meanwhile, approximately 12M illegal aliens[22] are already in the country and the U.S. government has little efficacy in tracking and deporting them. Based on recent executive directions for DHS not to enforce immigration laws,[23] deporting illegals may be even more constrained by political will than capacity. According to Department of Justice statistics, "Apprehensions for immigration violations peaked at 1.8 million in 2000 but dropped to 516,992 in 2010—the lowest level since 1972."[24] DHS' 2013 intercept goal that supports intercepts between the POEs is set at 352,000 illegals captured. That goal is a ~30 percent drop from the actual intercepts realized just two years ago. This reduced apprehension goal represents a disconnect between local and federal law enforcement desires. See Figure 6 to illustrate historical U.S. intercept rates.

---

[21] Arpaio and Sherman, *236*

[22] Jeremy Pelofsky, "Number of Illegal Immigrants in U.S. is Stable: DHS," *Reuters*, http://www.reuters.com/article/2012/03/24/us-usa-immigration-idUSBRE82N09I20120324, (accessed Mar 24, 2012).

[23] Stephan Dinan, "Homeland Security Suspends Immigration Agreements with Arizona Police," *Washington Times*, June 25, 2012.

[24] Mark Motivans, *Immigration Offenders in the Federal Justice System, 2010*, ed. James B. Lynch (Washington D.C.: US Government Printing Offices, 2012), 44.

Photo Removed Due to Copyright Restrictions

Figure 6-Illegal Apprehension along the U.S. Southwestern Border[25]

Mission 4: Safeguarding and Securing Cyberspace

The National Protection and Programs Directorate (NPPD) lead this mission[26] in

which it attempts to secure Executive Branch agencies' information technology and

hardware from cyber threats. DHS applies no tracked effort in this mission area to secure

the private sector cyberspace. Department efforts are largely inward focused to keep

DHS and the U.S. government running. DHS support goals include "monitoring for

intrusions and protecting other Cabinet-Level agencies" and " percent of external traffic

monitored for cyber intrusions at civilian Federal Executive Branch agencies..."[27] Since

most of cyberspace is owned by the private sector, DHS cannot be expected to manage

cyberspace activity or suppress this domain's adversary actors (wherever they sit).

---

[25] Adam Isacson and Maureen Meyer, *Beyond the Border Buildup: Security and Migrants Along the U.S.-Mexico Border* (Washington, D.C: Washington Office of North America, 2012), 3.
[26] NPPD is DHS's primary agency focused on protecting both physical and cyber infrastructures.
[27] U.S. Department of Homeland Security, *U.S. Department of Homeland Security Annual Performance Report 2011-13* (Washington D.C.: US Government Printing Office, 2011), 62.

However, because the majority of this domain is private and yet still vital to the American way of life, a better-informed private sector could better protect its assets and their equipment from harmful adversaries. As discussed in Chapter 2, hackers generally form their botnets by massing individual private-sector computers. Often these individual computers are leveraged because ignorant owners unknowingly comprised their own machines. After all, the U.S. government's cyber resiliency depends upon the private sector's systems, and much of the populace is dependent upon the government in their daily lives and in crisis.

Mission 5: Ensuring Resilience to Disasters

Federal Emergency Management Agency (FEMA) leads this mission area to bolster American resilience and preparedness but just focuses on natural disaster. However, as defined in the DHS strategic planning guidance, the threats are broader than just natural disasters; they include non-state actor threats as well. DHS surveyed Americans[28] to determine if U.S. citizens were adequately prepared for a crisis. This survey revealed that roughly one-third of the populace possessed a sense of preparedness and had taken some step to "prepare". DHS' current assessments mean that FEMA is within 10 percent of fully attaining its public preparedness goal. However, how well do the surveyed respondents truly understand the full spectrum of threats? The education and communication program at DHS' homepage lists a webpage for its current and past terrorist threat notices. These notices are used to keep the populace updated and informed.[29] However, there are no current or past notices posted there as of this thesis

---

[28] Ibid, 28.
[29] DHS' terrorist threat notice website is located at http://www.dhs.gov/national-terrorism-advisory-system.

writing. One could conclude that notices are not being generated. How well can the populace understand and prepare for the nation's adversary threats when there is no data provided by the authority responsible for the task? While the surveyed respondents may have felt that they were prepared, for what threats were they adequately educated to understand and consequently prepare?

Another education and informing effort promoting security and resiliency explores, "Percent of the U.S. population directly covered by FEMA connected radio transmission stations." This effort checks for DHS' ability to broadcast message(s) during crises. DHS sets their goal at 90 percent connectivity in non-crisis situations and has declared mission success in recent testing. However, testing during non-crisis periods will likely reach more of the populace than broadcasting in actual crisis periods. Even if DHS is able to broadcast during a crisis and transmit their critical information, the chances of reaching their 90 percent coverage threshold are unrealistic. The limiting reason is that during crises, many Americans will have little to no capacity to receive the transmission due to power outages, inoperable radios, and physical displacement from radios. Many first responders themselves may be similarly unfortunate and detached from broader response efforts. This excerpt from one Hurricane Katrina report illustrates the point that isolation from first responders and emergency-guidance information during a crisis appears increasingly likely:

> Six of eight police districts' operations were out of commission due to flooding, limiting (or precluding) their ability to establish command and control by performing basic law enforcement functions because their communications were destroyed. The lack of communications from those on the ground in the disaster zone and those coordinating the efforts in the

state and outside the state caused ineffective response to human suffering.[30]

Additional Gaps beyond DHS Missions

DHS prepared The National Preparedness Goal to develop approaches to create a resilient society in the face of the variety of threats facing America today. Although DHS is striving to protect the U.S., some areas remain gapped within their immediate pursuit. Those gaps were discussed in the previous section. The author also discovered some areas that fall outside of their current DHS purview worth considering. These gaps are discussed below.

Vertical Dominated Approach

The current approach to American resiliency uses a top-down approach where government rescues a needy populace. Little self-empowerment is addressed in DHS approaches to counter NSAs. This U.S. government approach to ensure American preparedness is comparable to the centralized, top-down approach used to secure the populaces in Iraq and Afghanistan.[31] The U.S. learned in both theaters that the populace was the center of gravity and that enduring solutions were better built from the bottom-up. The U.S. approach to its national preparedness might include the same realization.

While the top down approach is essential, it is insufficient in and of itself. Appending the current approach with a matching approach focused on micro-security

---

[30] Heather K. Meeds and Army War College (U.S.), *Communication Challenges during Incidents of National Significance: A Lesson from Hurricane Katrina* (Carlisle, PA.: U.S. Army War College, 2006), 9.

[31] The U.S. attempted to impose centrally developed governance solutions onto the populaces of both Iraq and Afghanistan shortly after the end of military operations. These efforts failed and progress toward establishing stability and security later arose from populace centric solution sets.

from the bottom up might afford greater resilience.[32] This approach could include

education on the threats and the historical realities of timely and adequate government

responses. Managing the populace's expectation for a government response can help

reduce associated angst if/when government responses do not resolve the populace's

needs. Lastly, reducing the populace's reliance and expectation for a quick government

response could moderate broad popular frustrations that could potentially endanger U.S.

government continuity of operations (COOP) and continuation of government (COG) in

severe catastrophes.[33]

Lack of a Comprehensive Approach

While DHS is the governmental department leading efforts for homeland security,

they are not earnestly coordinating their efforts with other departments. They currently

measure their success by addressing performance among missions exclusively within

their department.[34] The problem with this approach is that many of the effects needed to

attain their goals must be found outside DHS. For instance, the Department of Justice is

responsible for criminal investigation and security related intelligence inside the

country's borders. Developing measures that reinforce integration with these capabilities

could reinforce DHS's abilities in working its five mission areas.

Another example can be found in the Department of Treasury (DOT). DOT has

the primary capabilities for counter threat finance (CTF) and its authorities derive from

Executive Order 13324, titled *Blocking Property and Prohibiting Transactions with*

---

[32] U.S. National Research Council-Committee on Increasing National Resilience to Hazards and Disasters, *Disaster Resilience a National Imperative* (Washington, D.C.: National Academies Press, 2012), 15.

[33] Eric Raile, "The Microfoundations of Security and Implications for Governance" (Doctoral, Michigan State University, 2008), 17.

[34] U.S. Department of Homeland Security, *U.S. Department of Homeland Security Annual Performance Report* (Washington D.C.: US Government Printing Office, 2011), 8-37.

Persons Who Commit, Threaten to Commit, or Support Terrorism. CTF is a key component of fighting transnational organized crime and terrorists. Financially undermining NSAs is an ability far outside of DHS, but no measured program exists to build external approaches to leverage these capabilities. As described at the beginning of this thesis, NSA intent requires both capability and capacity to become a viable threat. Removing an organization's financial means can idle their capacities and render them an unviable threat to the U.S.. This approach can be an essential method to address an undeterrable NSA.

Overall, the current DHS approach is internally focused. The Department has been in existence since 2002, eleven years as of this writing. However, they are still wrestling with internal challenges of coordinating their missions among eight disparate subordinate agencies and the mission of implementing resiliency.[35]

Radicalization

DHS is not addressing radicalization as a counter measure to NSA threats. A key part of any extant threat is the actor's intent or willingness to do harm. DHS is currently focused on protecting the U.S. from adversaries by restricting their capabilities and capacities affording operational reach. A key oversight that exists is how to address the willingness and intent of one's adversaries to prevent them from doing any harm within the U.S. Within this gap are the particularly vulnerable risks from radicalized persons already inside the United States. These people can be U.S. citizens, legal or illegal immigrants.

---

[35] United States. Government Accountability Office, *Critical Infrastructure Protection: An Implementation Strategy could Advance DHS's Coordination of Resilience Efforts Across Ports and Other Infrastructure*, Government Printing Office, Washington, D.C..

AQ did not have to pass through any POEs to influence and activate MAJ Nidal Hassan; the internet connection was more than enough to radicalize him and motivate him to kill. He killed thirteen fellow service members and wounded 43 others in his November 5, 2009 attack at Fort Hood, Texas.[36] MAJ Hassan is a commissioned-Army officer who held a security clearance at the time of the attack. Meanwhile, there are still no DHS performance measures that focus on counter radicalization. When considering the efficacy of the POE versus illicit entry methods, it is also worth noting that the "Times Square car bomber" was also radicalized inside the U.S.. After radicalization, he both exited through POEs to attend terrorist training in Pakistan then returned through U.S. POEs and their associated TSA screenings without delay. While he carried no capacity for terror through the POEs, he returned with much more capability and intent. Radicalization is a policy area that remains unaddressed by DHS as it leads the effort to protect the U.S. homeland.

Pandemic Planning and Biological Threats

Current DHS approaches to secure the populace from pandemic disasters are unlikely to be successful based upon gaps in their timely distribution of prophylaxis. Biological hazards were discussed in chapters 2 and 3 and one can see how technology has increased the possibilities of non-state actors in recent years to create and either synthetic biological or bacterial weapons. This thesis also highlighted the risks of naturally-occurring epidemics and reviewed historical data from the 1918 Spanish Influenza epidemic to illustrate an epidemic's duration and destruction potential. During the 2009 H1N1 influenza epidemic, the US Department of Health and Human Services

---

[36] Office of the Secretary of Defense, *Protecting the Force: Lessons from FT Hood* (Ft. Belvoir: Defense Technical Information Center, 2010), 1.

found that "National-level surveillance information was often not sufficiently granular to characterize rapid changes in influenza-like illness or hospitalizations at the community level or to meet the information needs and demands of local responders and citizens."[37]

DHS is quite actively air sampling major U.S. cities for biological risks because minimizing response time from detection to prophylaxis distribution can be essential to survival. Untreated aerosolized-anthrax infections can kill in as little as 48 hours. Cutaneous anthrax exposure affords additional response time but still requires prophylaxis to prevent death.[38] Successful response to any discovered biological threat rest largely upon the timely distribution of prophylaxis that is produced, purchased, and stored under the Project Bioshield program. Project Bioshield incentivizes pharmaceutical manufacturers to produce large quantities of specific prophylaxis to be purchased and stored by DHS at strategic distribution centers around the country.[39] These distribution centers have been established to counter bacteria related attacks by ensuring that medications needed to combat botulin or anthrax will be readily available to the general public in a timely manner.

The challenges in these distribution scenarios come in their distribution planning. Argonne National Labs has performed distribution analysis for some of these centers to validate their distribution plans.[40] The planning assumptions going into these validation

[37] U.S. Department of Health and Human Services, *An HHS Retrospective on the 2009 H1N1 Influenza Pandemic to Advance all Hazards Preparedness* (Government Printing Office, Washington, D.C., 2012), iv.

[38] Center for Biosecurity of UPMC, *Bacillus Anthracis (Anthrax) Fact Sheet* (Pittsburg, PA: University of Pittsburg, 2011), 2.

[39] Congressional Research Service, *Project BioShield: Authorities, Appropriations, Acquisitions, and Issues for Congress: A Study Prepared Prepared for Members and Committees of Congress* by Congressional Research Service, July 2010 (Washington, D.C.: Government Printing Office, 2010), 4.

[40] Daniel Walsh and Chuck VanGronigen, "Logistics Modeling: Improving Resource Management and Public Information Strategies in Florida," *Journal of Business Continuity & Emergency Planning 5*, no. 3 (October 11, 2011), 1-9.

analyses are set around ideal scenarios. A response time goal from detection/exposure to personal medical attention is approximately two days. Receiving government-distributed medications in adequate time requires several preconditions, including awareness that the threat exists, and determination that one has been infected. Since distribution in ideal scenarios consumes nearly 48 hours[41] itself, the chances of a typical citizen understanding that they have been infected and receiving government distributed medicine within 48 hours is unlikely.

Other realistic planning criteria such as worker absenteeism, pharmaceutical hoarding, and infrastructure degradation were not considered in the scenarios proffered for distribution analyses.[42] Consequently, prophylaxis planning and operations are built upon faulty assumptions and currently accept considerable risk to achieve their missions. The U.S. populace is largely relying on a government-only provided remedy. A single solution approach places the populace at high risk for catastrophe. Further, Project Bioshield stocked-prophylaxes are bacterial oriented remedies and do nothing to mitigate viral threats that pose broader risks. Viral threats are far greater dangers than bacterial (e.g. anthrax) because they are self-replicating whereas bacterial threats are finite. DHS efforts countering bacterial threats do not consider non-pharmaceutical means that are affordable and available at the point of need. Preventative education and awareness could reduce the risks associated with both bacterial and viral threats.

Active Shooter

Another gapped risk that remains is the inability to deter active shooters and national policies that seemingly have little effect on attriting active shooter attack

---

41 Center for Biosecurity of UPMC, 2.
42 Daniel Walsh and Chuck VanGronigen, 6-7

capabilities. Regardless of incident titling—active shooter, work-place violence, and/or firearms-based terrorist attacks—these event types closely resemble one another. The results are usually quite similar as well, that is multiple unarmed citizens are shot to death and then shortly thereafter the shooter(s) terminate themselves.

If these attackers are truly undeterrable, then the best we can plan for is mitigation of these attacks. However, DHS has not championed counter measures for active shooters. An official investigation followed the FT Hood shootings and one key finding of the report states, "The initial response to the incident was prompt and effective."[43] This "effective response" has little bearing on deterrence, countering the threat, or resilience to withstand the threat. This response was relatively quick compared to typical active shootings but first responders are generally not relevant to preventing or surviving the attack. Numerous service members were already dead at the time of the initial emergency call and others expired while first responders were reacting. Therefore, improving response time to zero will ultimately not result in negating an attack and associated loss of life.

The DHS active shooter handbook describes the threat environment, offers ways to mitigate the risk, and states that resisting or fighting back against the shooter is to be avoided. The main themes of the pamphlet are, 1) to avoid being targeted, and 2) to wait for first responders. The problem with these approaches is that targeting is often random and most active shooter situations terminate themselves with no influence from law enforcement. Active shooter situations generally involve an enraged gunman who kills

---

[43] Office of the Secretary of Defense, *Protecting the Force*, 1.

indiscriminately for approximately three minutes then ultimately takes his own life.[44]

First responders generally arrive in five to ten minutes from the initial call for help.

Therefore, there appears to be little prescribed in the active shooter handbook to help

avoid either being in a shooting situation or expecting any help from first responders if

found in that situation.

Finally, although active shooters are a threat credible enough to warrant a DHS-

issued pamphlet on the topic, there remains no criterion in DHS' annual performance

plan for measuring the Department's performance for deterring active shooter risks on

either typical federal premises or any other public venues. Should numerous active

shootings recur, the DHS scorecard will still show a 100 percent success rate.[45]

---

[44] U.S. Department of Homeland Security, *Active Shooter: How to Respond* (Washington D.C.: U.S. Dept. of Homeland Security, 2008), 7.

[45] U.S. Department of Homeland Security, *U.S. Department of Homeland Security Annual Performance Report*, 10.

CHAPTER 6: RECOMMENDATIONS TO INCREASE AMERICAN RESILIENCE

"Although history doesn't repeat itself in detail, it does repeat in generalities."

Dr. Vardell Nesmith, PhD.

The U.S. is currently in an era similar to the 1949 period of its history. It is coming out of a long period of protracted war, its federal budget is a significant concern to the nation, and its adversaries are making unexpected moves. The U.S. must study the environment adequately to understand the realities of its capabilities and vulnerabilities. The U.S. must take that analysis and prepare for all of the possibilities it can afford. Accordingly, cheaper yet effective solutions are especially preferred.

This chapter will provide recommendations to address the threats discussed in the thesis and offers approaches to fill the gaps in the current top-down methodology. The areas to be addressed could ameliorate America's risks from TCOs, terrorists, ideologues as well as natural disasters while hardening the American populace both physically and psychologically from numerous threats. The next section illustrates recommendations for government centric approaches; populace centric approaches follow afterward.

Vulnerability Model

The previously described non-state actor threats (NSA) create a broad overlapping danger in which one NSA can pose several threats. This overlapping danger adds a level of complexity to developing a comprehensive approach to protection and resiliency. The author has built a matrix (see Figure 7) that highlights the potential threats from non-state actors, the level of impact posed by each type of attack, the difficulty to conduct the attack, the elements of government power required to mitigate these attack risks and the ability of the general populace to reduce risks associated with the attack type.

Threat	Environment			
	Level of Impact	Difficulty of Execution	Needed Govt Mitigation	Effect of Individual Action
Active Shooter	I	L	I, IN, L	H
Complex Attack	V	M	D, I, M, F, IN, L	M
Biological Attack	V	H	D, I, M, E, F, IN, L	H
Radiological Dispersal Device	V	H	D, I, M, F, IN, L	M
Cyber Attack	V	L	D, I, M, E, F, IN, L	H
Synthetic Viral Attack	S	M	D, I, M, E, F, IN, L	M
	Survival (S), Vital (V), Important (I), Peripheral (P)	Low (L), Medium (M), High (H)	Diplomatic (D), information (I), Military (M), Economic (E), Financial (F), Intelligence (IN), Law Enforcement (L)	Low (L), Medium (M), High (H)

Figure 7-National Vulnerabilities from Non-State Actor Attacks

The level of impact represents the intensity of national interest affected. The intensity of interests scale ranges from the highest interest to lowest interest respectively, that is, Survival, Vital, Important and Peripheral. Survival interest represents a threat that could result in the immediate destruction of one or more enduring nation interests. Vital interests represent immediate threats affecting national core interests. Important interests represent threats that will have an eroding or eventual effect upon national core interest.

Peripheral interests are the lowest concerns. These threats could result in some damage to American goals but not damage core interests.[1]

The level of difficulty represents the challenge that an NSA might face to execute a specific type of attack within the U.S. homeland. For instance, smuggling in a radiological dispersal device (RDD) requires much more effort and poses greater risk than conducting an active shooter attack. The author rates the RDD attack as high difficulty versus the low difficulty of an active shooter attack.

Government mitigation addresses the elements of national power required to mitigate the risks associated with the various kinds of attack. Some threat scenarios, such as cyber attacks, require considerable government effort and coordination to mitigate associated risks. This level of coordination is high because the nation (both government and populace) is so integrated through cyber means and so many different U.S. adversaries use this method against the U.S.. Active shooter scenarios are generally consequence management instead of deterrence, and are far less reaching in scope. Therefore, less government coordination is required surrounding this threat.

Ease of individual mitigation refers to positive steps individual citizens can take (e.g. education, preparedness) to reduce the risks posed by these various threats to themselves and/or broader American society. Some threats are easy to mitigate/negate with modest amounts of preparation and education. Threats with High (H) effect for individual action warrant examining in greater detail because multiple individual responses can aggregate into collective benefits thereby bolstering the resiliency desired in national approaches.

---

[1] Donald Edwin Nuechterlein, *America Overcommitted: United States National Interests in the 1980s* (Lexington, KY.: University Press of Kentucky, 1985), 10.

Understanding that limitations exists on what a resilient society can readily affect, the author recommends focusing on the threat areas listed in Figure 7 where the effect of individual action is "High." Although all threats are somewhat mitigated by individual action, the ones with "High" effect have the greatest effect. These attacks represent scenarios where American society can readily contribute to their own safety and the broader safety of other Americans. Though not in the High category for effective individual action, the author also recommends that synthetic-viral attack(s) be included as a focus area for a resilient society approach. This last recommendation is based upon the magnitude of potential destruction involved. Due to the survival level of impact, including the populace as part of the solution is prudent because they represent both the target and a potentially large part of the solution.

A resilient nation with a resilient populace would certainly have a positive effect on the collective approach to mitigating the many threats facing that nation. Given that resources available to U.S. government-pursued solutions are already stretched thin, exploring alternative approaches that increase security and resiliency make sense. There is value to consider approaches where the populace can participate in their own safety, and consequently, create a collective resiliency where the broader nation also realizes increased security. Specific approaches to mitigate the identified threats will be discussed in the following chapter.

Government Centric Approaches

Deterrence

A key part of any resiliency strategy is the ability to deter an adversary from attempting to harm us. This avoidance can come through both dissuasion and retribution considerations. For some adversaries, deterrence is not an option because their nefarious intentions are resolute. For these adversaries interdiction is the next escalated step of deterrence. These ideas are further discussed below.

Dissuasion and Retribution

Many U.S. adversaries pursue America's demise while limiting the potential of their own detriment. For these actors, the U.S. must display itself as a hardened target that is unlikely to suffer the damages they seek to deliver. More frequent national level exercises that reach further down into the municipalities and broader than a single-city event can demonstrate that the U.S. is organized enough to respond to attacks. The U.S. might consider including the populace in these exercises similar to the Israeli model discussed earlier in the thesis.[2] Creating a broader condition of awareness among the populace can increase national resiliency. Should U.S. national resiliency still not deter adversaries from attacking, then the U.S. must also show that any attempts at harming U.S. interests will be met with responses that greatly outweigh any potential gain they might pursue.

Interdiction

Information operations alone will not deter some adversaries, for these exceptional adversaries, force is applicable. "Since assuming office in 2009, President Barack Obama's administration has escalated targeted killings, primarily through an increase in unmanned drone strikes on al-Qaeda and Taliban leadership, but also through

---

[2] Israel regularly conducts homeland defense exercises to steel their populace against attacks. They have gone as far as to issue gas masks to their citizens to increase their resiliency.

an expansion of U.S. Special Operations kill/capture missions."[3] Given that these actors

are not covered by international law, they should be treated as subversives and saboteurs

within military operations and tribunals, or covert direct actions as required. However,

where the U.S. discerns undeterrable intent accompanied with both credible capability

and capacity, it should engage in lethal force to destroy the threat. The key threshold

here is that all three identified threat elements (discussed earlier)—intent, capability, and

capacity—must be present. Popular will supports this approach and a recent poll showed

that 53 percent of Americans support targeted killings, even killing of Americans abroad

who have been deemed as terrorists and show intent to harm America.[4] While targeted

killings have proven popular and effective in the cases like AQ leader Usama bin Laden,

broad political consequences must be considered in extraterritorial strikes when the

possibility to spoil an attack is also possible.

Countering Radicalization with Information Operations

A U.S. adversary's motivations may be religious, xenophobic, or socially driven.

Regardless of NSA motivation, information campaigns are the strategic weapons best

used for this fight because it limits the legitimacy of NSA causes. Using information

operations to highlight organizational hypocrisy and inconsistencies are particularly

damaging to the legitimacy of radical causes. NSAs such as LeT and al-Qaeda regularly

use new recruits who seek affirmation within their new terrorist organizations for the

most dangerous missions instead of leading the attack themselves. Another example

highlighting organizational hypocrisy among NSAs is found during Operation Iraqi

---

[3] Jonathan Masters, "Targeted Killings," *Backgrounder*, Counterterrorism (April 30, 2012), 2.
[4] ABC News, "Public Perceptions on Terrorism," www.polingreport.com,
http://www.pollingreport.com/terror.htm (accessed October 8, 2012).

Freedom (OIF). In OIF, Al-Qaeda in Iraq leaders often controlled suicide bombers from the comfort of luxury hotels and lavish compounds located in Syria.[5]

The U.S. government should seek a dialogue with habitually targeted recruitment-audiences to discuss perceived injustices that motivate potential recruits. Worldwide-target audiences have regularly included male youths and disgruntled minorities. The Mumbai attackers are one example of this target audience. In the U.S., target audiences often include prison populations.[6] By undermining NSA recruiting capacity, the U.S. also reduces both the capabilities derived from new recruits and the capacity to employ them. Wherever the U.S. can accomplish the taming of an adversary's motivation, it has increased its security.

Populace Centric Approaches

Much of the current top-down approaches for preparedness and resilience are focused within the governance channels but these approaches do not boldly embrace the very populace at risk. The populace and their safety are certainly an enduring national interest, but they are also a useful capability and capacity available to leverage in times of crisis. Given that it is fiscally and realistically impossible to deter every threat to the homeland, it is in the best interest of the U.S. to develop innovative approaches to mitigate the threats while also protecting the populace. Bottom-up approaches that embrace the populace to mitigate NSA threats are explored below.

---

[5] Congressional Research Service, *Iraq Regional Perspectives and U.S. Policy: A Study Prepared Prepared for Members and Committees of Congress* by Congressional Research Service, September 2007 (Washington, D.C.: Government Printing Office, 2007), 24.
[6] Mitchell D. Silber and Arvin Bhatt, *Radicalization in the West the Homegrown Threat* (New York, N.Y.: New York Police Dept., 2007), 32.

Long-Term Approaches to Countering DTOs/TCOs

DTOs/TCOs bring violence, destructive drugs, and dangerous persons into the

U.S. where these imports erode both the nation's welfare and security. One potential

long-term approach to reduce TCO/DTO threats includes demand reduction and its

subsequent reduction in illicit revenue. TCOs and their subset of Drug Trafficking

Organizations are businesses; bankrupting a business is the most permanent way of

eradicating it. Attriting the inflows of currency to these types of organizations quickly

erodes their operational reach that harms U.S. interests.

Currently, 72 percent of the U.S. counter narcotic effort (based on budgeting) is

interdiction focused and 28 percent is treatment; this is a gross imbalance.[7] Creating a

demand reduction is a more systemic approach to attack the problem but that would

require an open and honest dialogue about America's drug consumption problem.

Preventing future users is far more economical than treating addicts afterwards. An

information campaign aimed at elementary school students that show the hard realities of

drug use is worth the effort. Images such as the "faces of meth"[8] (See Figure 8) resonate

with younger students and teenagers.[9] While current treatment programs should endure,

stopping the next generation from ever becoming users should go far toward reducing

demand, and over time, the associated profits that empower DTOs/TCOs.

---

[7] Office of National Drug Control Policy, *National Drug Control Budget-FY 2012 Funding Highlights, Executive Summary* (Washington, D.C.: Government Printing Office, 2011), 1.

[8] Bret King and Curtis Saunders, "Faces of Meth," Multnomah County Sheriff's Office;, http://www.facesofmeth.us (accessed November 1, 2012).

[9] T. M. Siebel and S. A. Mange, "The Montana Meth Project: 'Unselling' a Dangerous Drug," *Stanford Law & Policy Review.* Volume 20, Issue 2, (2009), 405.

Photo Removed Due to Copyright Restrictions

Figure 8 Physical Results of Methamphetamine Use[10]

It is envisioned the costs of these media campaigns should be a fraction of current

U.S. interdiction efforts because they can be distributed-based learning and enhanced

with available local law enforcement and volunteer recovered addicts. Since these young

students' choices are in the future, the avoidance programs will be unable to show

immediate results. This delay in result is often a challenge for programs struggling for

part inclusion in the federal budget.

To date, the U.S. has been fighting battles instead of a coherent campaign against

drugs. Some government sources report that narcotic interception is capturing roughly 2

percent of traffickers' revenue.[11] The current approach of countering narcotics through

interception has proven ineffective when measured by the interception rates and the fact

that drug demand is continually increasing in the U.S..[12] If the U.S government

successfully doubled its current interdiction rates, it will still be only scratching at the

overall narcotics problem and interdicting less than 5 percent of the money returning to

---

[10] King and Saunders, "Faces of Meth", 1

[11] U.S. Immigration and Customs Enforcement's "National Bulk Cash Smuggling Center," US Department of Homeland Security, www.ice.gov/bulk-cash-smuggling-center (accessed October 8, 2012).

[12] Congressional Research Service, *Southwest Border Violence Issues in Identifying and Measuring Spillover Violence A Study Prepared Prepared for Members and Committees of Congress* by Congressional Research Service, June 2011 (Washington, D.C.: Government Printing Office, 2011), 7.

the DTOs/TCOs. Reflecting on the long history of black market prostitution illustrates that when a demand signal exists in the market place, there will be an associated market supplier who seeks profits from that transaction. Education to reduce the market demand is key to reducing these illicit revenues.

By reducing the revenues flowing to TCOs/DTOs, one also reduces capacities of TCOs along with their presence and associated influences within the US. Reduced income also reduces TCO/DTO ability to sell those illicit capacities to other threat actors who also have nefarious intentions towards the U.S. and its populace. Reducing the "commodification" is a significant step towards breaking the threats posed by terrorists and non-state actors. Reducing the funding streams of TCOs/DTOs also reduces the operating capital of terrorist actors who reap benefits from narcotics trafficking.

Cyber Education

To counter the cyber threat, the U.S. government should lead a comprehensive education campaign to inform its public of destructive-cyber actors and their associated risks. The Zeus virus[13] stole over $70M from private users and is just one example of a litany of malware out there. Only 5 percent of passive malware is effective but spear phishing and other user-involved attacks exceed 60 percent effectiveness.[14] Spear phishing requires ignorance to succeed and deceiving the user is a key component to reaping huge increases in attack effectiveness. This technique is a huge component to building the botnets used in Directed Denial of Service attacks.

---

[13] The Zeus virus targets Windows based machines with a trojan horse style virus that logs the keystrokes of targeted users as they perform banking transactions. This information is then relayed back to the cyber terrorists who leverage the newly gained account information to steal money from the compromised bank account.

[14] Mark Bowden, *Worm: The First Digital World War* (New York: Atlantic Monthly Press, 2011), 36.

Education costs relatively little compared to consequence management and it is the main protection against these threats. Since the majority of the internet infrastructure is private, prevention might be the best the government can do. However, given the heavy U.S. economic and individual investment/reliance on the cyber domain for business and daily functioning, it is imperative that the private sector be hardened and resilient to cyber threats. Cyber is another area of potential cooperation and collaboration between the U.S. government and the private sector that should be further explored to increase national resiliency.

Active Shooters

Active Shooters endeavor to kill whomever they desire at the particular moment of their attacks. These shooters consistently kill in areas of little resistance such as schools, federal facilities, and college campuses where law-abiding citizen are legally forbidden to carry firearms themselves. This policy is the standard for most federal property from post offices to military installations. For instance, even though all service members are expressly trained to use firearms proficiently and many have extensive background checks and resultant security clearances, federal law (USC 18-930) forbids these members to carry personal firearms onto federal property. This situation reflects a logic trap that is truly ironic because existing policies seemingly do not directly address the problem; instead, they appear to target only law-abiding citizens. The result is an armed adversary that is empowered to continue to commit this act.

The active shooter is clearly not willing to submit to the law and current policies have proven inadequate to prevent the attacker from their assault. The U.S. government—and state governments where applicable—should develop policies that define standards to become "qualified" for carrying firearms. Affording those qualified individuals the legal ability to carry firearms into these currently "gun free zones" can: 1) provide deterrence against attackers who seek a soft target; and, 2) quickly de-escalate an attack and save precious lives long before the first responders arrive to begin consequence management.

All Hazards Approach[15]

FEMA regularly uses education programs to encourage people to be situationally aware of natural threats around them but leaves threats from NSAs unaddressed in their education programs for "preparedness." Current preparedness programs address weather events like hurricanes or other natural disasters such as earthquakes and wild fires. Typical recommendations include ensuring one has batteries for a flashlight and radio, and drawing potable water for use and consumption in the case of utility services outages. These recommendations are appropriate for short duration disasters that accompany weather events but are not adequate when the crisis duration lasts weeks.

Long-duration threats such as pandemics and biological attacks can be mitigated with personal preparation similar to the weather threats FEMA already addresses. However, education and prior planning is essential to mitigate these threats. For instance, pandemics tend to spread through human-to-human contact. Simple non-pharmaceutical measures like social distancing (remaining six feet apart from others potentially infected),

---

[15] All Hazards Approach is a term originating with the *Pandemic and All-Hazards Preparedness Act* passed into law on Dec. 19, 2006 and its purpose is "to improve the Nation's public health and medical preparedness and response capabilities for emergencies, whether naturally occurring, accidental, or deliberate."

routine hand washing with anti-bacterial soaps, and keeping hands away from one's face are viable methods to reduce spreading contagious diseases.[16]

Pandemics have been shown to last for long periods. Quarantines during the 1918 Spanish Influenza outbreak lasted for several weeks.[17] A quarantine of several weeks in today's just-in-time based society could be ruinous. Today, people may be faced between two methods of death in this scenario—infection or starvation. Planning for longer periods with appropriate provisions to support lengthy sequester/quarantine is a course of action that does not have to be economically burdensome. Tax incentives, such as sales tax holidays on preparation items, could incentivize proactive planning and help the populace with these purchases and at the same time, prepare for other short-term natural disaster events mentioned in the previous section. Increased resilience in this area is easily attainable but the populace must understand the potential threats and their associated risks.

Counter Argument

Arguments against these recommendations often center on the ideas that national problems are too large for the populace to manage and require government action. While that perspective is partly correct, it is mostly wrong. National problems are so large that government alone cannot solve them. Current efforts are overwhelmingly a top-down approach from the federal government down to local municipalities, and stop there except for occasional weather warnings.

---

[16] Howard Markel, Harvey Lipman, and J. Alexander Navarro, "Nonpharmaceutical Interventions Implemented by US Cities during the 1918-1919 Influenza Pandemic," *Journal of American Medicine*, no. 6 (August 8, 2007), 644.

[17] Eric Allely, *National Response to Biologic Contagion: Lessons from Pandemic Planning* (Suffolk, VA: Joint Center for Operational Analysis, 2008), 15.

The problems the U.S. faces need solutions with all available capabilities applied. *The Project for National Security Reform, Volume I* broaches the idea of horizontal integration across the interagency;[18] this author recommends that the U.S. must better engage the populace as well. The American populace is the last echelon of capabilities and can truly increase its resiliency by decreasing its external dependence. When government efforts fail to deter, then the American populace is truly the first responder on the scene. Community actions from natural disasters to Flight 93 passengers[19] illustrate this resiliency truth. While government involvement is essential for general protection of the population, it remains insufficient to deter all threats. Further, as seen through numerous natural disasters, the government alone is unable to achieve the resiliency it seeks.

---

[18] Richard Weitz and James Locher, *Project on National Security Reform Case Studies Volume I* (Washington, D.C.: Project on National Security Reform; Center for the Study of the Presidency, 2008), 61.
[19] On 9/11, the passengers on United Airlines flight #93 attacked their plane's hi-jackers and gave their lives to protect the nation at a point when the government could protect neither them or itself.

CHAPTER 7: CONCLUSIONS

Non-state actor threats are steadily increasing in strength due to advances in technology, collusion, globalization, and ever-growing illicit monies that buy nefarious cooperation and hardware. Meanwhile, existing gaps in the current government approaches are expanding as resources to counter NSAs are increasingly constrained. The government should consider new approaches to embrace the populace that include 1) increasing the public awareness of the threats, 2) educating the populace on ways to mitigate the threats, and 3) creating resiliency policies founded on facts instead of emotions.

Countries such as China and Israel regularly incorporate their citizens as part of their overall national security approaches and the U.S. should follow their example. The Department of Homeland Security (DHS) already engages the American populace in its approach to improve resiliency against natural disasters; including the populace's support against NSAs is a logical next step.

Americans have learned that non-state adversaries need not first defeat their government before attacking them. Commodification enables NSAs through illicit means to bypass government countermeasures and reach Americans directly. This thesis has illustrated the increasing risks posed by non-state actors to American society. As previously discussed, technology advances have been shown to improve adversarial capabilities while globalization and "commodification" have expanded their capacity or operational reach.

Illicit collaborating among NSAs towards disparate ends has, at times, been both witting and unwitting. Arguments that disparate strategic objectives among NSAs will preclude their collusion have been shown to be false. Invested motives or consented collusion are not prerequisites for exchanging the capabilities and capacities needed to cause significant disruption and destruction to American society. Independent actors, sometimes without malicious intentions, greatly increase Americans' risks to catastrophic destruction. Academic ego among the scientific community drove this community to release sensitive synthetic-biology information to the world. This information greatly increases risk for a catastrophic attack.

Psychological effects have been illustrated to be at least as dangerous to American society as an original destructive event; at times over-reactions can actually cause greater damage than the initial attack itself. Mere disruption can have cascading effects on American society and its way of life. Creating prepared mindsets that resist dangerous over reactions is essential to limit cascading effects addressed earlier.

The U.S. government actively works to assure its enduring security interests, and pursuing resiliency is one way to further that effort. However, the government is approaching its national preparedness too slowly within DHS. Further, the government approach is imbalanced by using a predominately top down approach towards resiliency and not embracing the American populace as a full team member.

The diverse threats described in this thesis demonstrate that NSA threats are too broad for the government to prevent completely. In a fiscally constrained environment, policy makers need to be especially wise about the approaches taken to reduce American risks and increase national resiliency. The government can and should focus on the longer-term security and resiliency goals; however, Americans should be embraced and encouraged to increase their support for more immediate and local security goals.

This thesis' recommendations illustrate population centric approaches towards response and preparedness that also improves horizontal resiliency across U.S. society. This type of grass roots resiliency provides immediate resources at the point of need and strengthens the vertical resiliency approach currently pursued by DHS. Horizontal resiliency does not replace the current vertical approach; rather, it strengthens that approach. Lastly, because recommended approaches are largely awareness, education, and policy based approaches, these additional approaches should be relatively inexpensive compared to current vertical approaches.

Americans' risks from NSA attacks are growing but much of the populace is unaware of the risks. Because of the ignorance involved with NSA threats, few Americans are resilient in the face of an attack. If the federal government fails to reduce the population's expectations of what it can provide while the risks of attack steadily increase, the government should expect significant psychological impacts, public outrage and psychological disruption when the next attack occurs. This mindset could erode U.S. government legitimacy and its ability to govern. The American government should fully inform the populace of potential risks, help them prepare to counter these risks and rely upon them as partners resisting NSA threats.

APPENDIX A – GLOSSARY

- Active Shooter: An individual using firearms to kill or attempting to kill people in a confined and populated area; in many cases, little warning or predictability is afforded to the targeted victims.

- All Hazards Approach: A single strategy or plan that addresses mitigation methods for several potential crises.

- Commodification: The ability of an organization to procure capabilities or capacities from another organization (both licit and illicit) through outsourcing. This approach reduces the challenges of developing internal capacities and allows limited means to be focused on an organization's essential tasks and missions, all the while, expanding the reach and abilities on the contracting organization. [1]

- Complex Attack: An attack using combined arms or multiple weapon systems within a single assault or operation.

- Deoxyribonucleic Acid (DNA): The basic hereditary building material in humans and almost all other organisms.[2]

- Drug Trafficking Organization (DTO): A collection of likeminded persons engaged in the trafficking of illicit narcotics for profit. Generally, the term DTO is reserved for the largest of the traffickers instead of street-level retailers.

---

[1] Phillip Bobbitt, *Terror and Consent: The Wars for the Twenty-First Century* (New York, N.Y.: Knopf, Alfred A, 2008), 672.

[2] National Library of Medicine, "Genetics Home Reference Sheet," National Institute of Health, http://ghr.nlm.nih.gov/handbook/basics/dna (accessed September 7, 2012).

- Ideologue: One who adheres to a belief or conviction, often on faith alone. In the case of religion, standards of behavior are often prescribed. For the non-religious, actions and motivations can be more capricious.

- Mortality Rate: The rate at which death results from contraction of a specific disease.

- Nation State: A sovereign territory recognized by the international community with a government and established borders. Inhabitants/citizens generally have some common history or culture that binds them together within the state's borders.

- Non-State Actor: An entity that resides within a nation state or states but is not governed and often not limited by the national government(s) where it resides.

- Resilience: "The ability of an entity—asset, organization, community, region —to anticipate, resist, absorb, respond to, adapt to, and recover from a disturbance."[3]

- Super Empowered Individual: A person who has reached a significant level of potentially harmful capacity. Means of empowerment might come through technology and or finances.

- Synthetic Biology: "…an innovative and growing field that unites engineering and biology. It builds on the powerful research that came about as a result of a recombinant DNA technology and genome sequencing."[4]

---

[3] L. Carlson et al., *Resilience: Theory and Applications* (Chicago, Illinois: Argonne National Labs, 2012), 1.

[4] U.S. National Academies-Futures Initiative, "Synthetic Biology: Building on Nature's Inspiration; Interdisciplinary Research Team Summaries; Conference" (Beckman Center, Irvine, California, National Academies Press, November 20, 2009).

- Terrorism: The unlawful use of violence or threat of violence to instill fear and coerce governments or societies. Terrorism is often motivated by religious, political, or other ideological beliefs and committed in the pursuit of goals that are usually political.[5]

- Transnational Criminal Organization (TCO): An entity that operates illicit businesses across nationally recognized borders. These groups are profit driven but often have some links to ideological causes.

- Virulence: The capacity of a virus to transmit itself from one host to another by overcoming the immune defenses of that host.

---

[5] U.S. Joint Chiefs of Staff, *Department of Defense Dictionary of Military and Associated Terms*, ed. Joint Doctrine Division, Vol. 2012 (Washington, D.C.: Government Printing Office), November 2012, 29.

BIBLIOGRAPHY

ABC News. "Public Perceptions on Terrorism." www.pollingreport.com. http://www.pollingreport.com/terror.htm (accessed October 8, 2012).

Aday, Sean. *Blogs and Bullets II New Media and Conflict After the Arab Spring*. Washington, D.C.: United States Institute of Peace, 2012.

Allely, Eric. *National Response to Biologic Contagion: Lessons from Pandemic Planning*. Suffolk, VA: Joint Center for Operational Analysis, 2008.

Army National Guard-Stand to Magazine. "Army National Guard Operation Phalanx." United States Army. http://www.army.mil/article/56819/Army_National_Guard_Operation_Phalanx/ (accessed January 17, 2013).

Arpaio, Joe, and Len Sherman. *Joe's Law: America's Toughest Sheriff Takes on Illegal Immigration, Drugs, and Everything Else that Threatens America*. New York, N.Y.: AMACOM, 2008.

Associated Press. "Phone Transcripts of Mumbai Attacks Indicate Gunmen Not Acting Alone Fox News." Fox News. www.foxnews.com/story/0,2933,477424,00.html (accessed October 29, 2012).

Associated Press. "Colombia Rebels Linked to Mexico Drug Cartels." New York Times. http://www.nytimes.com/2008/10/08/world/americas/08mexico.html (accessed January 4, 2013).

Barrett, Devlin. "Retaliation Fears Spur Anonymity in Internet Case." *Wall Street Journal -Eastern Edition,* January 28, 2012.

Bhugra, Dinesh. Yuval Neria, Raz Gross & Randall Marshall (Editors) (2007). "9/11: Mental Health in the Wake of Terrorist Attacks." *International Review of Psychiatry* 22, no. 2 (April, 2010): 224-5.

Bobbitt, Phillip. *Terror and Consent: The Wars for the Twenty-First Century*. New York, N.Y.: Alfred A Knopf, 2008.

Bongar, Bruce Michael. *Psychology of Terrorism*. New York, N.Y.: Oxford University Press, 2007.

Bowden, Mark. *Worm: The First Digital World War*. New York, N.Y.: Atlantic Monthly Press, 2011.

Burke, D. K. "Moore's Law Graph." http://www.dreamviews.com/f77/moores-law-there-limit-98762/ (accessed October 29, 2012).

Carlson, L., G. Bassett, W. Buehring, and M. Collins. *Resilience: Theory and Applications*. Chicago, IL: Argonne National Labs, 2012.

Cengage Learning. "The Economic Impact of 9/11." Gale World Headquarters. http://behindtheheadlines.info/teaching911/the-economic-impact-of-911-interactive-chart-dow-jones-industrial-average.php (accessed November 10, 2012).

Censer, Jack and William Miller. *On the Trail of the D.C. Sniper: Fear and the Media.* Charlottesville, VA: University of Virginia Press, 2010.

Center for Biosecurity of UPMC. *Bacillus Anthracis (Anthrax) Fact Sheet.* Pittsburg, PA: University of Pittsburg, 2011.

Center for Strategic Leadership. *The Hybrid Threat: Crime, Terrorism and Insurgency in Mexico.* Washington D.C.: George Washington University and U.S. Army War College, 2011.

Centers for Disease Control and Prevention. "Interim Pre-Pandemic Planning Guidance Community Strategy for Pandemic Influenza Mitigation in the United States: Early, Targeted, Layered use of Nonpharmaceutical Interventions." Centers for Disease Control and Prevention. http://www.pandemicflu.gov/plan/community/community_mitigation.pdf (accessed October 9, 2012).

Certified Genetool. "For Sale: ABI 3900 Oligo (DNA) Synthesizer." http://www.labx.com/v2/adsearch/detail3.cfm?adnumb=481442 (accessed November 8, 2012).

Cohen, John and Martin Enserink. "One of Two Hotly Debated H5N1 Papers Finally Published." ScienceNow. http://news.sciencemag.org/sciencenow/2012/05/one-of-two-hotly-debated-h5n1-pa.html (accessed September 4, 2012).

Congressional Research Service. *Mexico's Drug Trafficking Organizations Source and Scope of the Rising Violence, August 2012.* Library of Congress, Washington, D.C.: Government Printing Office, 2012.

Congressional Research Service. *Presidential Policy Directive 8 and the National Preparedness System Background and Issues for Congress, October 2011.* Library of Congress, Washington, D.C.: Government Printing Office, 2011.

Congressional Research Service. *Southwest Border Violence Issues in Identifying and Measuring Spillover Violence. February 2011.* Library of Congress, Washington, D.C.: Government Printing Office, 2011.

Congressional Research Service. *Project BioShield: Authorities, Appropriations, Acquisitions, and Issues for Congress. June 2010.* Library of Congress, Washington, D.C.: Government Printing Office, 2010.

Congressional Research Service. *The National Response Framework: Overview and Possible Issues for Congress. November 2008.* Library of Congress, Washington, D.C.: Government Printing Office, 2008.

Congressional Research Service. *Iraq Regional Perspectives and U.S. Policy, October 2007.* Library of Congress, Washington, D.C.: Government Printing Office, 2007.

Cornish, Paul and Royal Institute of International Affairs. *On Cyber Warfare.* London, U.K.: Chatham House, 2010.

Cullen, David. *Columbine.* New York, N.Y.: Grand Central Publishing, 2009.

Committee on Homeland Security, Subcommittee on Cybersecurity, Infrastructure Protection and Security Technologies. *Subcommittee Hearing: Hearing on Draft Legislative Proposal on Cybersecurity.* Congressional Hearing, 112th Cong., 1st sess., December 6, 2011.

Committee on Foreign Affairs, Subcommittee. *Combating the Haqqani Terrorist Network.* 112th Cong., 2nd Sess., September 13, 2012.

Committee on Science, Engineering, and Public Policy. *Disaster Resilience: A National Imperative,* Committee on Increasing National Resilience to Hazards and Disasters, Washington, D.C.: National Academies Press, 2012.

De Amicis, Albert. "Los Zetas and La Familia Michoacana Drug Trafficking Organizations (DTOs)." Masters thesis, University of Pittsburg, 2011.

Diaz, Tom and Barbara Newman. *Lightning Out of Lebanon: Hezbollah Terrorists on American Soil.* New York, N.Y.: Ballantine Books, 2005.

Dickson, Keith. *Justifying War in a Globalized World: Problems and Prospects.* Norfolk, VA: National Defense University, 2011.

Dinan, Stephan. "Homeland Security Suspends Immigration Agreements with Arizona Police." *Washington Times.* June 25, 2012.

Dunlop, John. "The September 2004 Beslan Terrorist Incident-New Findings." *Center on Democracy, Development, and the Rule of Law Working Papers*, no. 115 (July, 2009): 3-6. http://iis-db.stanford.edu/pubs/22577/No_115_Dunlop_Beslan_2004.pdf (accessed November 10, 2012).

Dyer, Geoff. "US Bolsters Security After Libya Raid." Financial Times. http://www.ft.com/cms/s/0/e8d91afe-fc53-11e1-aef9-00144feabdc0.html (accessed October 29, 2012).

English, T. J. *Havana Nocturne: How the Mob Owned Cuba– and then Lost it to the Revolution.* New York, N.Y.: William Morrow, 2008.

Farah, Douglas. *Transnational Organized Crime, Terrorism, and Criminalized States in Latin America; an Emerging Tier-One National Security Priority.* Carlisle, PA: U.S. Army War College, 2012.

Farah, Douglas and Stephen Braun. *Merchant of Death: Money, Guns, Planes, and the Man Who Makes War Possible.* Edited by Navta Associates Inc. Hoboken, N.J.: John Wiley & Sons, 2007.

Federal Bureau of Investigation. "FBI 100-the Unabomber." Department of Justice. https://www.fbi.gov/news/stories/2008/april/unabomber_042408 (accessed September 15, 2012).

Fletcher, Holly. *Aum Shinrikyo.* Council on Foreign Relations. http://www.cfr.org/japan/aum-shinrikyo/p9238 Council on Foreign Relations, 2012. (accessed on

Frantz, Ashley. "The Haqqani Network, a Family and a Terror Group." CNN. www.cnn.com/2012/09/07/world/who-is-haqqani/index.html (accessed January 4, 2013).

Freed, Joshua. "iPhone 5 Sales: Many U.S. Stores Reportedly Sold Out of the Device Already." *Huffington Post*, September 12, 2012.

Freedom House. "Freedom on the Net: Bahrain." Freedom House. http://www.freedomhouse.org/report/freedom-net/2012/bahrain (accessed October 29, 2012).

Friedman, Thomas. *The World is Flat: A Brief History of the Twenty-First Century*. 1st rev. and expanded edition. New York, N.Y.: Farrar, Straus and Giroux, 2006.

Garthoff, Douglas F. *Directors of Central Intelligence as Leaders of the U.S. Intelligence Community*. Washington, D.C.: Potomac Books Inc., 2005.

Gecowets, Gregory and Jefferson Marquis. "Applying the Lessons of Hurricane Katrina." *Joint Forces Quarterly* 48 (First Quarter, 2008).

Goodman, Joshua. "Colombia Probes FARC Ties to Uranium Seized in Bogota." Bloomberg.com http://www.bloomberg.com/apps/news?pid=newsarchive&sid=a2kQfcdqP.ns (accessed September 30, 2012).

Gilligan, Gregory. "Looming Storm Prompts a Run on Grocery Stores." *Richmond Times-Dispatch.* January 16, 2013.

Groundspeak Incorporated. "Groundspeak's Geocaching Application." Geocaching.com. http://www.geocaching.com/live/ (accessed October 29, 2012).

Hamilton, Lee and Thomas Kean. *Tenth Anniversary Report Card the Status of the 9/11 Commission Recommendations*. Washington, D.C.: Bipartisan Policy Center, 2011.

Hobfoll, Stevan E., Robert J. Johnson, Brian J. Hall, Patrick A. Palmieri, Daphna Canetti-Nisim, and Sandro Galea. "Trajectories of Resilience, Resistance, and Distress during Ongoing Terrorism: The Case of Jews and Arabs in Israel." *Journal of Consulting & Clinical Psychology* 77, no. 1 (February 2009):138-148.

Hoffman, Gil. "Hezbollah Drone Photographed Secret IDF Bases." Jerusalem Post. http://www.jpost.com/Defense/Article.aspx?id=287724 (accessed December 13, 2012).

International Business Times. "UN Network Compromised for Two-Years by Unknown Foreign Power: Are Anonymous Hackers Helping the World Get Serious about Cyber Crime?" *International Business Times*, August 3, 2011.

Isacson, Adam and Maureen Meyer. *Beyond the Border Buildup: Security and Migrants Along the U.S.-Mexico Border*. Washington, D.C: Washington Office of North America, 2012.

Johnson, David V. "Assessing the Impact of Employee Absenteeism on Emergency Operations during a Pandemic." Masters thesis, National Fire Academy, 2008.

Kaplan, Robert. *Monsoon: The Indian Ocean and the Future of American Power*. New York, N.Y.: Random House, 2010.

Kilcullen, David. "Counterterrorism Blog Panel: The 2008 Mumbai Attacks." Distributed on-line, Counter Terrorism Blog, posted December 4, 2008. http://counterterrorismblog.org/upload/2008/12/The%202008%20Mumbai%20Attacks_CTB%20Event%2012.04.08.pdf. (accessed August 12, 2012)

Killebrew, Robert, Matthew Irvine, and David Glaser. "A New U.S.-Colombian Relationship: Transnational Crime and U.S. National Security." *Orbis* 56, no. 2 (2012).

King, Bret and Curtis Saunders. "Faces of Meth." Multnomah County Sheriff's Office;. http://www.facesofmeth.us (accessed November 1, 2012).

Kiser, John W. "Terrorism and our Domestic Peril." The Eisenhower Institute. www.eisenhowerinstitute.org (accessed September 18, 2012).

Klimburg, Alexander. "Mobilising Cyber Power." *Survival -London- International Institute for Strategic Studies* 53, no. 1 (February 2011):41-60.

Korb, Lawrence J. and Alexander Rothman. "No First use: The Way to Contain Nuclear War in South Asia." *Bulletin of the Atomic Scientists* 68, no. 2 (March 2012):34-42.

Liang, Qiao and Wang Xiangsui. *Unrestricted Warfare*. Beijing, CN: PLA Literature and Arts Publishing House Arts, 1999.

Lesperance, A. and J. Miller. *Preventing Absenteeism and Promoting Resilience among Health Care Workers in Biological Emergencies*. Washington, D.C.:2009.

Longmire, Sylvia. "Mexican DTO Influence Extends Deep into United States." *CTC Sentinal* 5, no. 7 (July 2012):16.

Longmire, Sylvia. "Why Border Violence Spillover Needs to be Defined." *Homeland Security Today*, January 17, 2012: 1-2.

Markel, Howard, Harvey Lipman, and J. Alexander Navarro. "Nonpharmaceutical Interventions Implemented by US Cities during the 1918-1919 Influenza Pandemic." *Journal of American Medicine* 298, no. 6 (August 8, 2007): 644-645.

Mansour, Essam. "The Role of Social Networking Sites (SNSs) in the January 25th Revolution in Egypt." *Library Review* 61, no. 2 (2012): 128-135.

Masters, Jonathan. "Targeted Killings." *Backgrounder*. (April 2012) http://www.cfr.org/counterterrorism/targeted-killings/p9627 (accessed August 12, 2012)

Mastropiero, Danielle. "Hezbollah Uses Fauxtography to Sway Public." International Media Ethics. http://www.imediaethics.org/News/411/Hezbollah_uses_fauxtography_to_sway_public_.php (accessed October 30, 2012).

Mazzetti, Mark and Shane Scott. "Evidence Mounts for Taliban Role in Bomb Plot." *New York Times*, May 5, 2010.

Mazzetti, Mark, Shane Scott, and Alissa Rubin. "Brutal Haqqani Crime Clan Bedevils U.S. in Afghanistan." *New York Times*, Sept 24, 2011.

McCardle, Shelley and H. Rosoff. *The Dynamics of Evolving Beliefs, Concerns Emotions, and Behavioral Avoidance Following 9/11: A Longitudinal Analysis of Representative Archival Samples*. Boston, MA: National Institute of Health, 2012.

Mena, Tony. "Mexico: Our Next AOR?" *The Foreign Affairs Officers Journal* XIV, no. 2 (May 2011):10-12.

Meeds, Heather K. "Communication Challenges during Incidents of National Significance: A Lesson from Hurricane Katrina." Carlisle, PA: U.S. Army War College, 2006.

Middle East Reporter. "United Lebanese Army: Attempts to Keep it So." *Middle East Reporter (Weekly Edition)* 137, no. 1227 (November 2010) http://ezproxy6.ndu.edu/login?url=http://search.ebscohost.com/login.aspx?direct=true&db=bwh&AN=55229667&site=ehost-live&scope=site (accessed September 8, 2012).

Miller, Judith. "Qaeda Videos Seem to Show Chemical Tests." *New York Times*, August 19, 2002.

Monahan, Tom and Mark Stainbrook. "Learning from the Lessons of the 2008 Mumbai Terrorist Attacks." *Police Chief* 78, no. 2 (2011):25-32.

Motivans, Mark. *Immigration Offenders in the Federal Justice System, 2010*. Federal Justice Statistics Program. Edited by James B. Lynch. Washington D.C.: US Government Printing Offices, 2012.

Naím, Moisés. *Illicit: How Smugglers, Traffickers and Copycats are Hijacking the Global Economy*. New York, N.Y.: Doubleday, 2005.

National Drug Intelligence Center. *National Drug Threat Assessment, 2011*. Washington, D.C.: US Department of Justice, 2011.

National Gang Intelligence Center. *National Gang Threat Assessment 2011: Emerging Trends*. Washington, D.C.: National Gang Intelligence Center, 2011.

National Library of Medicine. "Genetics Home Reference Sheet." National Institute of Health. http://ghr.nlm.nih.gov/handbook/basics/dna (accessed September 7, 2012).

Nuechterlein, Donald Edwin,. *America Overcommitted: United States National Interests in the 1980s*. Lexington, KY.: University Press of Kentucky, 1985.

O'Connell, Mary Ellen. "Enhancing the Status of Non-State Actors through a Global War on Terror?" *Columbia Journal of Transnational Law* 43, no. 2 (January 2005):435-458.

Office of National Drug Control Policy. *National Drug Control Budget-FY 2012 Funding Highlights, Executive Summary*. Washington, D.C.: Government Printing Office, 2011.

Office of the Secretary of Defense. *Protecting the Force: Lessons from FT Hood*, by Anthony Cain. Defense Technical Information Center, Ft. Belvoir, VA, 2010.

Office of the Secretary of Defense. *Sustaining U.S. Global Leadership: Priorities for 21st Century Defense, by Leon Panetta.* Washington, D.C.: Government Printing Office, 2012.

Olson, Kyle. "Aum Shinrikyo: Once and Future Threat?" *Emerging Infectious Diseases* 5, no. 4 (August 1999). http://wwwnc.cdc.gov/eid/article/5/4/99-0409_article.htm (accessed September 12, 2012)

Padilla, Carlos. "The FARC and Hugo Chavez is Contemporary Venezuela a Threat to Colombia?" Masters thesis, Naval Postgraduate School, 2010.

Pelofsky, Jeremy. "Number of Illegal Immigrants in U.S. is Stable: DHS." *Reuters,* March 24, 2012.

Perdue, Jon B. *The War of all the People: The Nexus of Latin American Radicalism and Middle Eastern Terrorism.* Washington, D.C.: Potomac Books, 2012.

Project on National Security Reform and The Center for the Study of the Presidency. "Forging a New Shield." Washington, D.C., Center for the Study of the Presidency, 2008.

Rabasa, Angel. *The Lessons of Mumbai.* Santa Monica, CA: RAND Corp., 2009.

Raile, Eric. "The Microfoundations of Security and Implications for Governance." PhD. Diss., Michigan State University, 2008.

Rajghatta, Chidanand. "Rana, Headley Implicate Pak, ISI in Mumbai Attack during ISI Chief's Visit to US." *Times of India,* April 12, 2011.

Reidel, Bruce. "The Al Qaeda-Iran Connection." Brookings Institute. http://www.brookings.edu/research/opinions/2011/05/29-al-qaeda-riedel (accessed October 29, 2012).

Rose, Ananda. "Death in the Desert." *New York Times,* June 22, 2012.

Sasaki, Sayo. "Aum Victim Keeps Memory Alive Via Film." *Japan Times on-Line.* http://www.japantimes.co.jp/text/nn20100309f1.html (accessed September 20, 2012)

Schmitt, Eric. "Aafia Siddiqui." *New York Times,* September 24, 2010.

Schneck, Phyllis. "McAfee Advocates using Global Attack Information Sharing to Counter Growing Cyber Threats to Critical Infrastructure and the American Economy." *Business Wire (English),* March 16, 2011. http://www.businesswire.com/news/home/20110316006621/en/McAfee-Advocates-Global-Attack-Information-Sharing-Counter (accessed October 20, 2012).

Schubert, Atika. "WikiLeaks Releases Entire Archive of U.S. Embassy Cables." *CNN World.* http://articles.cnn.com/2011-09-02/world/us.wikileaks_1_diplomatic-cables-wikileaks-embassy-cables?_s=PM:WORLD (accessed September 13, 2012).

Schulden, Jeffrey, Jieru Chen, Marcie-jo Kresnow, Ileana Arias, Alexander Crosby, James Mercy, Thomas Simon, Peter Thomas, John Davies-Cole, and David Blythe. "Psychological Responses to the Sniper Attacks: Washington DC Area, October 2002." *American Journal of Preventive Medicine* 31, no. 4 (October 2006).

Seper, Jerry and Matthew Cella. "Signs in Arizona Warn of Smuggler Dangers." *Washington Times*, August 31, 2010.

Siebel, T. M. and S. A. Mange. "The Montana Meth Project: "Unselling" a Dangerous Drug." *Stanford Law & Policy Review* 20 (2009):405-416.

Silber, Mitchell D. and Arvin Bhatt. *Radicalization in the West the Homegrown Threat.* New York, N.Y.: New York Police Dept., 2007.

Smith, Adam and Edwin Cannan. *The Wealth of Nations.* New York, N.Y.: Modern Library, 2000.

Steinhardt, Bernice and Marcia Crosse. *Influenza Pandemic Lessons from the H1N1 Pandemic should be Incorporated into Future Planning.* Washington, D.C.: U.S. Govt. Accountability Office, June 27, 2011.

Stern, Jessica. *Terror in the Name of God: Why Religious Militants Kill.* New York, N.Y.: Ecco, 2003.

Stewart, Scott. "The Perceived Car Bomb Threat in Mexico." STRATFOR. http://www.stratfor.com/weekly/20110413-perceived-car-bomb-threat-mexico (accessed October 29, 2012).

Sullivan, John. "Counter-Supply and Counter-Violence Approaches to Narcotics Trafficking." *Small Wars & Insurgencies* 21, no. 1 (2010):179-195.

Trenchard, Terence. *Hezbollah in Transition: Moving from Terrorism to Political Legitimacy.* Carlisle, PA: U.S. Army War College, 2011.

Tsu, Sun. *The Art of War.* Translated by J. J. L. Duyvendak and Hanzhang Tao. Penguin Classics Deluxe Edition. London, U.K.: Wordsworth, 1998.

U.S. Army-Center for Army Lessons Learned. "Stability Operations in the Western Hemisphere: Observations, Insights, Lessons." Fort Leavenworth, KS: Center for Army Lessons Learned, 2011.

U.S. Assistant to the President for Homeland Security and Counterterrorism. "The Federal Response to Hurricane Katrina: Lessons Learned." White House. http://georgewbush-whitehouse.archives.gov/reports/katrina-lessons-learned/ (accessed December 13, 2012).

U.S. Department of Energy. *Preventing Absenteeism and Promoting Resilience among Health Care Workers in Biological Emergencies.* Washington, D.C.; Government Printing Office, 2009.

U.S. Department of Health and Human Services. *An HHS Retrospective on the 2009 H1N1 Influenza Pandemic to Advance all Hazards Preparedness.* Washington, D.C.: Government Printing Office, 2012.

U.S. Department of Homeland Security. *National Emergency Communications Plan 2008.* Washington D.C.: Government Printing Office, 2008.

U.S. Department of Homeland Security. *Department of Homeland Security Strategic Plan Feb 2012.* Washington, D.C.: Government Printing Office, 2012.

U.S. Department of Homeland Security. *National Preparedness Goal*. Washington, D.C.: Government Printing Office, 2011.

U.S. Department of Homeland Security. *U.S. Department of Homeland Security Annual Performance Report*. Washington, D.C.: U.S. Government Printing Office, 2011.

U.S. Department of Homeland Security. *Active Shooter: How to Respond*. Washington D.C.: U.S. Department of Homeland Security, 2008.

U.S. Department of Justice (National Drug Intelligence Center). *National Drug Threat Assessment 2010*. Washington, D.C.: U.S. Department of Justice: National Drug Intelligence Center, 2010.

U.S. Department of State. "Report to Congress on the Haqqani Network http://www.state.gov/secretary/rm/2012/09/197474.htm (accessed September 20, 2012).

U.S. General Accounting Office. *Critical Infrastructure Protection: Efforts of the Financial Services Sector to Address Cyber Threats*. Washington, D.C.: U.S. General Accounting Office, 2003.

U.S. General Accounting Office. *Critical Infrastructure Protection: An Implementation Strategy could Advance DHS's Coordination of Resilience Efforts Across Ports and Other Infrastructure*. Washington, D.C., Government Printing Office, 2012.

U.S. Congress. House. Committee on Homeland Security. *Hezbollah in the Western Hemisphere: Hearing before Subcommittee on Counterterrorism and Intelligence*. 112th Cong., 1st sess., July 7, 2011.

U.S. Congress. House. Subcommittee on Counterterrorism and Intelligence. *Iranian Terror Operations on American Soil: Hearing before Subcommittee on Counterterrorism and Intelligence*. 112th Cong., 1st sess., October 26, 2011.

U.S. Congress. House. Committee on Homeland Security. *Iran, Hezbollah, and the Threat to the Homeland. Hearing before: House Committee on Homeland Security*. 112th Cong., 2nd sess., March 21, 2012.

U.S. Immigration and Customs Enforcement. "National Bulk Cash Smuggling Center." US Government. http://www.ice.gov/bulk-cash-smuggling-center (accessed October 8, 2012).

U.S. Joint Chiefs of Staff. *Capstone Concept for Joint Operations 2020*. Washington, D.C.: Joint Chiefs of Staff, October 2012.

U.S. Joint Chiefs of Staff. *Decade of War. Volume I, Enduring Lessons from the Past Decade of Operations*. Suffolk, VA: Joint Staff J7-Joint and Coalition Operational Analysis, 2012.

U.S. Joint Chiefs of Staff. *Department of Defense Dictionary of Military and Associated Terms*. JP 1.02. Washington, D.C.: Joint Chiefs of Staff, 2012.

U.S. Joint Chiefs of Staff. *Capstone Concept for Joint Operations 2009*. Washington, D.C.: Joint Chiefs of Staff, 2009.

U.S. Joint Chiefs of Staff. *Joint Publication 1.0, Doctrine for the Armed Forces of the United States*. Washington, D.C.: Joint Chiefs of Staff, 2009.

U.S. Joint Chiefs of Staff. *Super Empowered Threat Brief*. Suffolk, VA: Joint Staff J7-Joint Center for Operational Analysis, 2008.

U.S. National Academies-Futures Initiative. "Synthetic Biology: Building on Nature's Inspiration; Interdisciplinary Research Team Summaries; Conference." Irvine, CA: National Academies Press, November 20, 2009.

U.S. National Research Council (Committee on Increasing National Resilience to Hazards and Disasters). *Disaster Resilience a National Imperative*. Washington, D.C.: National Academies Press, 2012.

U.S. President. *National Security Strategy*. Washington, D.C.: Government Printing Office, May 2010.

U.S. President. *PPD-8: National Preparedness*. Washington, D.C.: Government Printing Office, March 2011.

Von Clausewitz, Carl and Thomas J. Cutler. "On War." *U.S. Naval Institute Proceedings* 135, no. 1 (January 2009): 68.

Walsh, Daniel and Chuck VanGronigen. "Logistics Modeling: Improving Resource Management and Public Information Strategies in Florida." *Journal of Business Continuity & Emergency Planning* 5, no. 3 (October 11, 2011): 1-12.

Williams, Phil and Felbab-Brown, Vanda. "Drug Trafficking, Violence, and Instability." Carlisle, PA., U.S. Army War College. 2012.

Woodhill, James. "Cyber Security Advocate James R. Woodhill Presented Problems and Solutions Related to Commercial Account Cyber-Theft." BusinessWire.com. http://www.businesswire.com/news/home/20120604006209/en/Cyber-Security-Advocate-James-R.-Woodhill-Presented (accessed November 16, 2012).

Woodward, Bob. *Obama's Wars*. New York, N.Y.: Simon & Schuster, 2010.

Ziegler, John J. *"From Beirut to Khobar Towers: Improving the Combating Terrorism Program."* Maxwell Air Force Base, AL.: Air Command and Staff College, 1998.

www.ingramcontent.com/pod-product-compliance
Lightning Source LLC
Chambersburg PA
CBHW080309290526
45790CB00005B/1975